Chalk Talk Made Easy

By William Allen Bixler

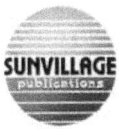

www.sunvillagepublications.com

Chalk Talk Made Easy
By William Allen Bixler

Copyright © 2011

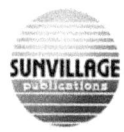

www.sunvillagepublications.com

Cover design by www.WebCopyAlchemy.com

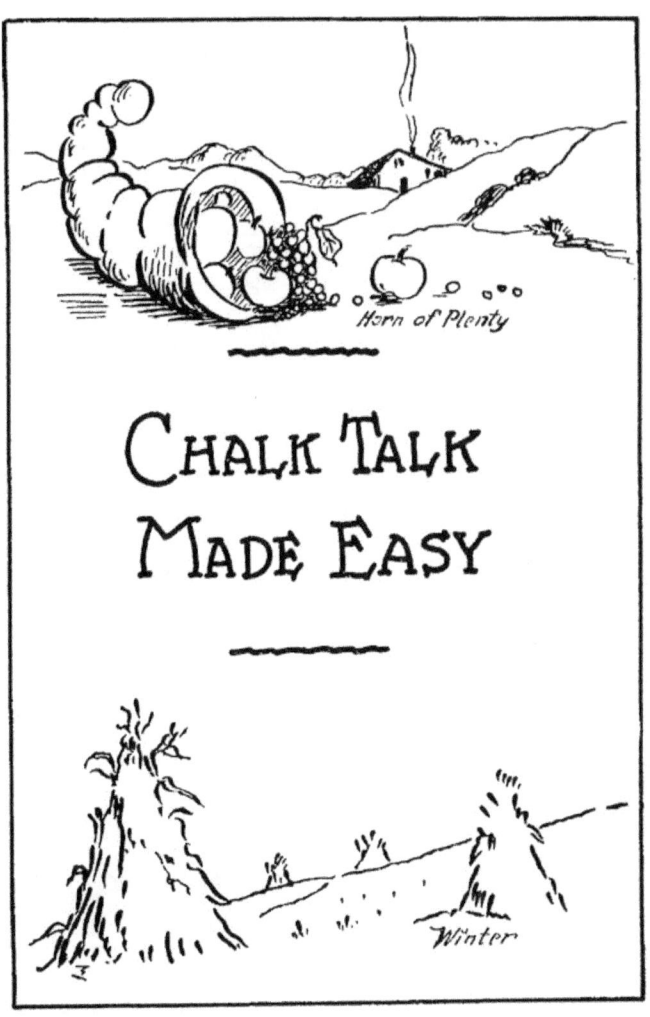

Horn of Plenty

Chalk Talk
Made Easy

Winter

In writing this book the author had in his mind constantly the thought of helpfulness to the beginner.

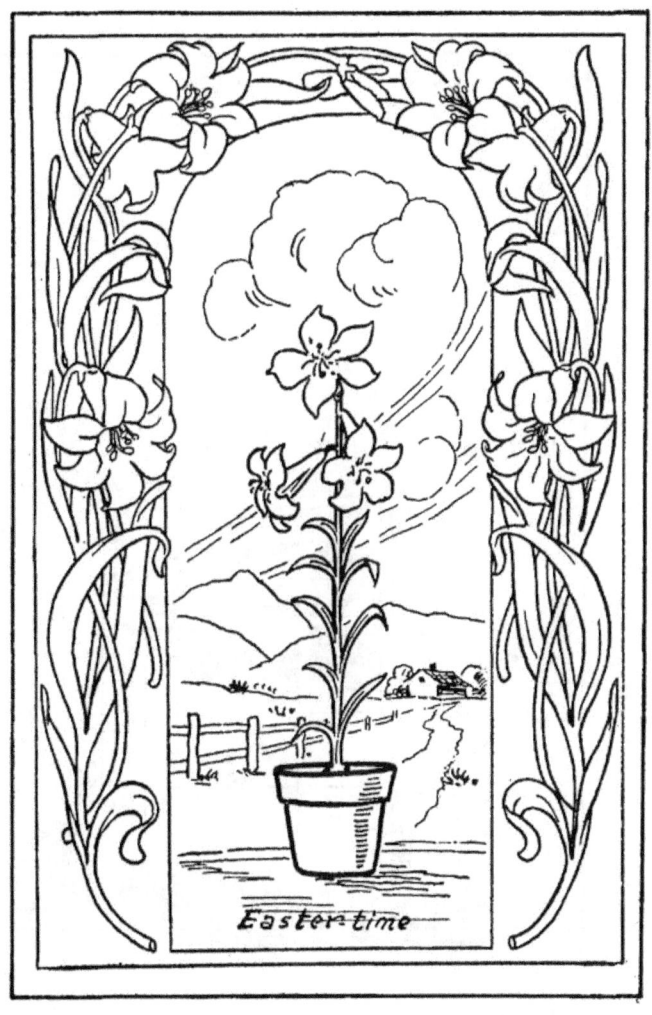

Easter-time

A good subject for Easter. You can use only a portion of the flowers if you want them. Color the background so as to leave the lily white. Lilies signify purity.

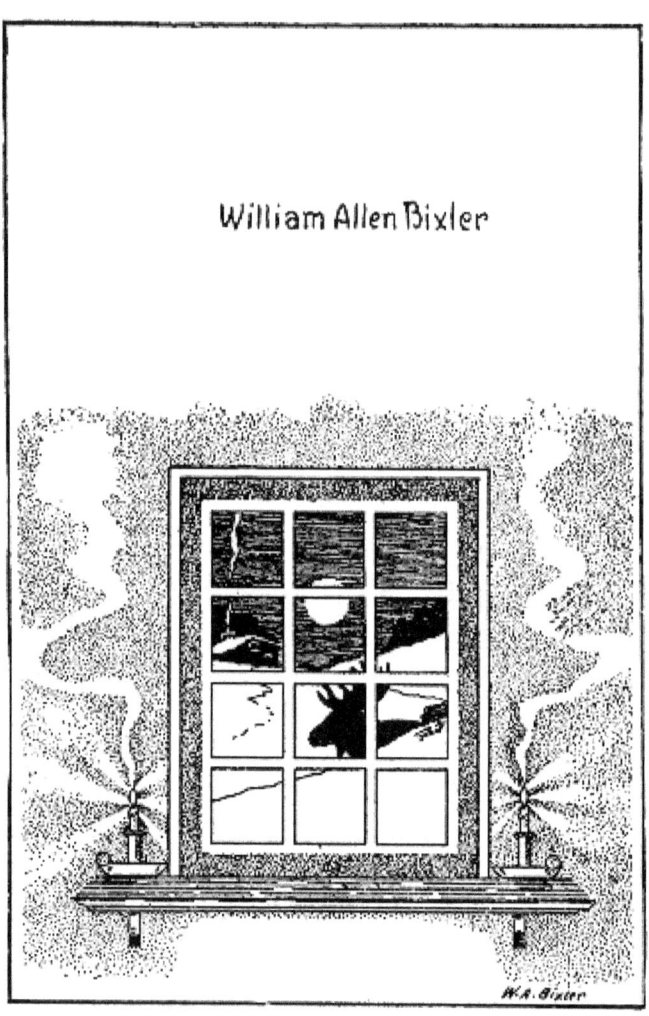

One does not need to be an artist to use the crayon successfully. Chalk talking is an art in itself, and by a little practice any speaker can increase his ability 100 per cent.

THE AUTHOR

William A. Bixler, the artist-author, has produced at his easel a crayon sketch of the boy Christ kneeling on the seashore, his face toward the rising sun, imploring his heavenly Father for assistance to prepare himself for his lifework, unmindful of the cross reflected in the shadow on the sand.

Mr. Bixler, a devout father, has always shown a keen interest in children and young people. He has written hundreds of articles and nature stories for publication and is also the author of books having a large circulation. For years he has demonstrated the use of crayon at religious and social gatherings.

The title of "Riley Artist" was given Mr. Bixler for his work in connection with paintings of James Whitcomb Riley's "Old Swimmin' Hole" and the life-size bronze statue of Riley erected in Greenfield, Ind., in 1918. It was in 1912 that Mr. Bixler produced a painting in oil of the famous spot for the poet Riley. Then a committee of Greenfield citizens determined to erect a bronze statue in honor of Mr. Riley and they retained Mr. Bixler to make oil paintings of the "Old Swimmin' Hole" for schools throughout the Union that would contribute toward the monument fund. During the following six years over 5,000 canvases of the noted spot were produced for that purpose by Mr. Bixler, the "Riley Artist."

The Anderson (Ind.) *Herald,* November 26, 1918, said of Mr. Bixler: "Without any question, Mr. Bixler has more paintings hanging in the schools of the United States than any other living artist."

The Long Beach (Calif.) *Telegram,* 1927, says: "The outstanding feature of Mr. Bixler's program is his drawing. In a few moments he transforms a blank canvas into a charming landscape. Mr. Bixler is an artist of national fame, known particularly for his painting of the "Old Swimmin' Hole'."

CONTENTS

LIST OF ILLUSTRATIONS

WHERE TO FIND NECESSARY INFORMATION

Drawing Board—for permanent use in a classroom or home—details of how to make and how to use, pages 20 and 22.

Folding Combination Board and Easel—different kinds for different purposes, illustrated and explained on page 21.

Crayons—what kind to use, what to call for, and where to purchase, page 26.

Colors—what kind to use, and where to use them, pages 58 to *64.*

Paper—proper color, sizes, kind, and where to purchase, page 26.

Tools and Equipment—other than already mentioned; also valuable hints on how to protect clothing and hands, pages 40 to 46.

Lighting Equipment, when needed for special work and occasions, illustrations and sketch, page 21.

Blending Colors—to soften tones and blend, also to tint the entire picture, pages 26 and 28.

First Practice Sketches—characters representing the human form, page 39-

Simplified Sketches—drawing for the beginner, pages 23, 25, 27, 29, 31, 35, and 37.

Sketches of the Eye, page 85; *Ear,* page 89; *Nose,* page 87; and *Mouth,* page 87.

Hands in Many Shapes—a very necessary part of your chalk-talk program. Practice these much. Pages 75, 77, 79, and 81.

Planning a Program—valuable suggestions on how to select and what to select from the many sketches in this book, pages 52 to 58.

Suggested Program—for different occasions, pages 56 and 58.

Surprise and Turn-Over Pictures—the most interesting of any kind of sketches before the public. Pages 65 and 127.

Enlarging a Picture to Any Size—how to copy and enlarge—its principles by a simple process, pages 32 and 33.

Lettering—how to make different styles of lettering correctly, and the principles, pages 98 to 103.

Sunday-School Program—what to use in planning a picture before your class. Sketches and hints on your program, pages 72 to 86.

Religious Programs—for young people's and general church services, there is a wealth of material in chapters "Symbols and Their Meaning" and "Crayon in the Sunday School." There is much material in these chapters for Easter or Christmas programs.

Smiles and Frowns and Different Facial Expressions—in chapter "Drawing the Human Form" and in many sketches throughout this book.

Closing or Good-Night Numbers—page 128.

CHALK TALK MADE EASY

AN INTRODUCTION

OLD and young, of every tribe and nation, find in pictures a universal language that arrests attention and rivets interest. Through the open eye, which *is* said to be the open window of the soul, principles of right and spiritual truth enter.

Chalk talk is nothing more nor less than the quick manipulation, or execution of crayon sketches, pictures, or diagrams which illustrate to the observer the points which the speaker wishes to convey.

While many of those who follow commercial, professional, educational, religious, and social chalk talk seek primarily to entertain, yet most of them use the same tactics to impress serious and wholesome problems.

The main secret in chalk talk lies in the fact that the audience sees the picture grow by every line, their curiosity is aroused and they are constantly held in expectation till the final result.

Many persons have held back from using the chalk and crayon because they have not known that the principles are within their very grasp, and principally for that reason the author desires to inspire each and every person who is interested, to develop this art.

This book is not purposely intended for any particular vocation or class of people; but there seems to be a great need of it among Sunday-school teachers and workers with young people, for chalk talk affords many opportunities of impressing the youth with lessons of truth. The worker among young people will find herein a world of undeveloped resources in his vocation.

Any person who desires to develop his ability as a chalk talker will find here the cream of principles necessary for such development. It simplifies the principles and explains all necessary details in such a way that any person, whether he has any inclination or qualifications along the line of drawing or not, can make use of this undeveloped power in teaching, or as an entertaining feature, and can by a little practice start chalk talking himself.

Success will come to him who desires to apply himself to this work, just the same as it has come to others, if he will go at it with a determination to succeed and a willingness to practice—and then practice some more. No matter what your vocation or present pursuit may be, there is some use to which you can put your crayon to advantage. It can be more easily adapted to certain callings than to others; but no matter what line of endeavor you follow or how crude your first attempts may be, the main item of success is to make a beginning—not next year, or next month, or next week, but now. The book in your hand will not only help you get started, but it may be the first foundation stone in a successful chalk talk career.

The sketches are put in this book for use. If practiced carefully, they will surprise the diligent student with their practical value. They have come from observation, public entertainers, friends, books, magazines, years of study and experience, and from chalk talkers' demonstrations.

I have drawn nearly all the illustrations myself, to assist the student in securing the desired results. The greater part of these sketches and ideas are not original with me. I have selected many of them from a collection gathered here and there over a period of years and have forgotten the true source of most of them.

In my years of practice and study, I have absorbed many ideas and practical working sketches from various sources, especially from some splendid books on art and chalk talking by the following authors: B. J. Griswold, H. T. Bailey, R. F. Y. Pierce, Ella N. Wood, Florence H. Darnell, Charles H. Bartholomew, Manuel Rosenberg, Edna A. Foster, E. C. Matthews, Wade H. Smith, Harlan Tarbell, Chas. Lederer, and others.

WILLIAM ALLEN BIXLER

Anderson, Ind.

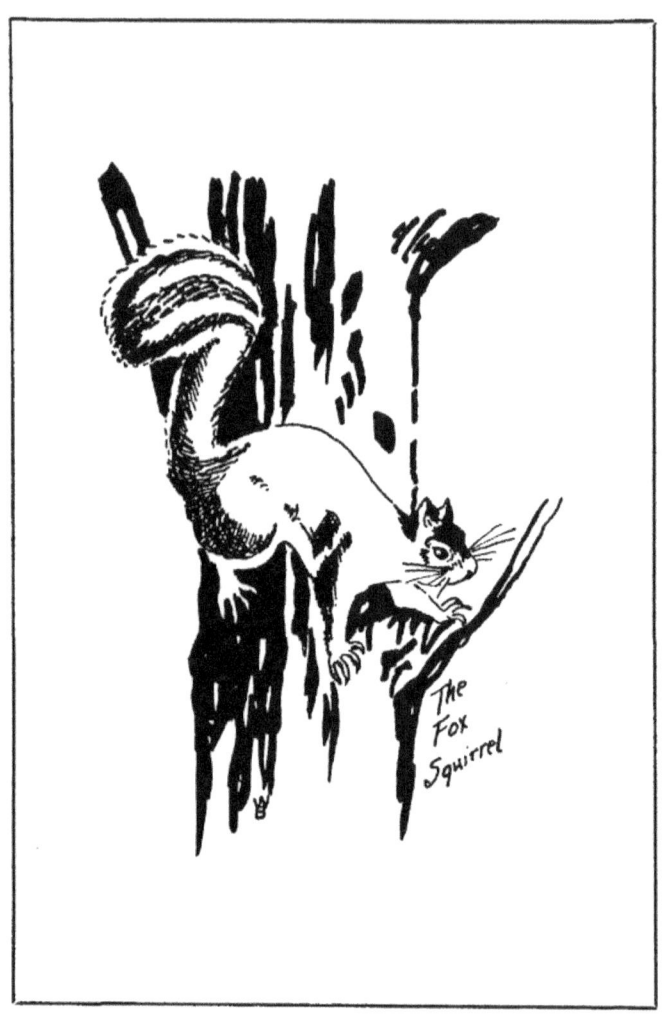

CHALK TALK MADE EASY

CHALK PICTURES APPEAL TO ALL AGES

Chalk picture programs are more often given for the benefit of the older people, but young folks and children seem to enjoy them with even greater interest.

I have found, while doing public illustrating, that the little child will sit almost breathless, his eye following every move of the hand. At the same time the older person will display no less interest and will sit perfectly still with eyes, ears, and mouth open—taking in the entire situation.

The older person may look on the drawing in a critical way, whereas the child will take in the entire picture. What the drawing lacks, the child's imagination will supply; in fact, the child's imagination is one of his greatest assets. This is demonstrated by the broomstick he uses for a horse and his scores of other make-believe ways of amusement.

In order to see a demonstration of the creative powers of the child, watch the little girl as she plays with her doll. That the doll has life and is her very own child, and that she as the doll's mother bears the same relationship toward it as her own mother bears toward her, goes without question; the domestic interests of her father's family are lived out in her own little creative mind and life.

The development of a picture stimulates the creative imagination in the child's mind. As the different marks are made, the child is eagerly awaiting every movement to see if the picture will develop into what he thought it would be when finished.

17

The impression is therefore made on the child's mind, as well as on the paper or blackboard. If each mark representing a character in your story is briefly explained as the picture is made, by the time the drawing is complete the impression is indelibly fixed on the mind of the child; and even if the drawing be ever so crude, the creative imagination of the child's mind is satisfied. It is for this reason that the person who uses the chalk need not try to draw perfectly, from an artistic standpoint. Direct a child's mind toward the creative, and you you have given him that which will be of greater help and a larger incentive to work than any other one thing.

The strongest impressions on a child's mind are made through the eye and the imagination. The chalk talk will not only appeal, but will shape the imaginations into realities. Since the child's mind is active and restless, the merest suggestion produces an effect; and whether this effect is good or bad, it rests with the chalk talker.

It is necessary, then, that our drawings represent in a general way what we are trying to picture. Only essentials should be drawn, and the lines should be done with a firm, confident hand, even though they are mere outlines of crude objects.

With all the child's imagination he might be able to see in a straight line that which represents a man; but a body, head, arms, and legs will enable the child more easily to recognize the object, and he will be better pleased. Also, the child can visualize the running or walking position when we draw the figure inclined forward and the legs bent at the knee; and the features of the face can be made to express the emotions. A good-natured or jolly countenance can easily be expressed by curving the corners of the mouth up; the man with the sour look, or "down in the mouth," is shown by having the corners of the mouth turned down.

The essential of a girl or woman is a dress. Each object should have the general features so plainly drawn that it will

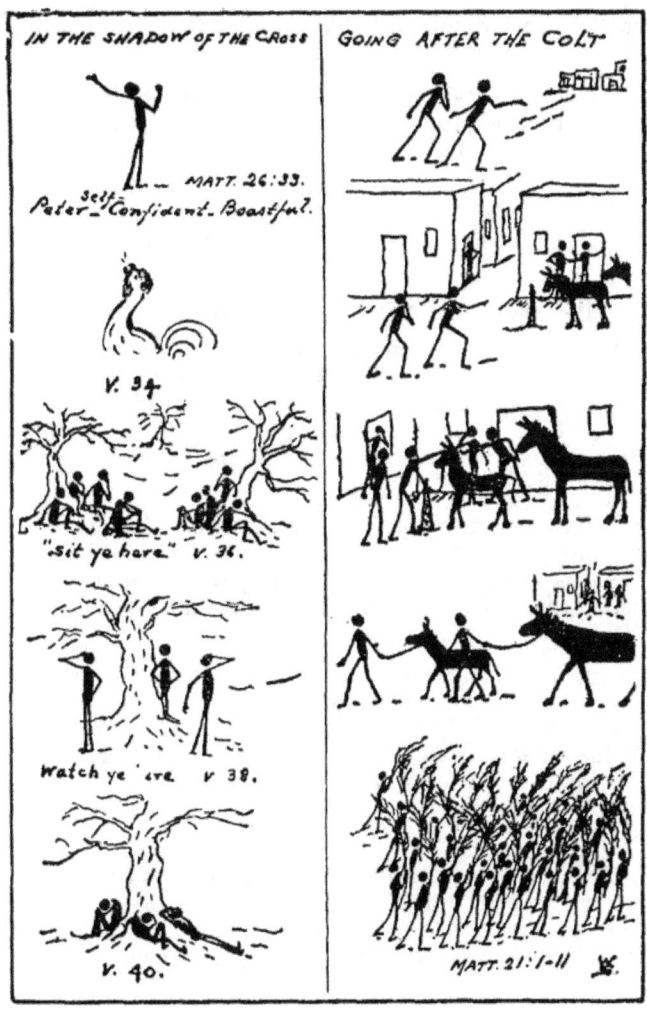

Wade Smith's style of illustrating a Sunday-school lesson. Reproduced by permission of Sunday School Times Company. (Copyrighted.) See page 39 for other characters.

not be necessary to place a title underneath telling what it is intended to be.

We should let every line and curve count for something that is essential to the picture; but we are more likely to draw too much than too little.

HOW TO MAKE A DRAWING BOARD

There are a number of ways in which you can make a drawing board or easel to hold your drawings.

For home practice nothing is better than a drawing board of convenient size made of matched lumber. It is better to have it a little larger than necessary than too small. It should be almost exactly the size of the paper used. It should not be less than 24x36 inches; even a larger board is better for general public work.

It must be perfectly smooth, and cleats on the back to hold it flat should be fastened with screws from the back. Any little unevenness or crack will show on your picture, especially if the defect comes in a place where a solid mark is to be made.

A good drawing board may be made of smooth builders' board, or wallboard, as some call it. Any lumber company or firm handling building materials can supply this for you. Do not get a pebbled or rough surface. The only objection to builders' board is that there is a possibility of warping; but this can be overcome by giving both sides a coat of paint or shellac before the atmospheric elements start the warping process.

You can make a portable work easel, such as chalk talkers use, out of strong canvas or 10-ounce duck for the background, with a device to stretch it perfectly tight each way. A portable easel that can easily be carried where wanted and erected in

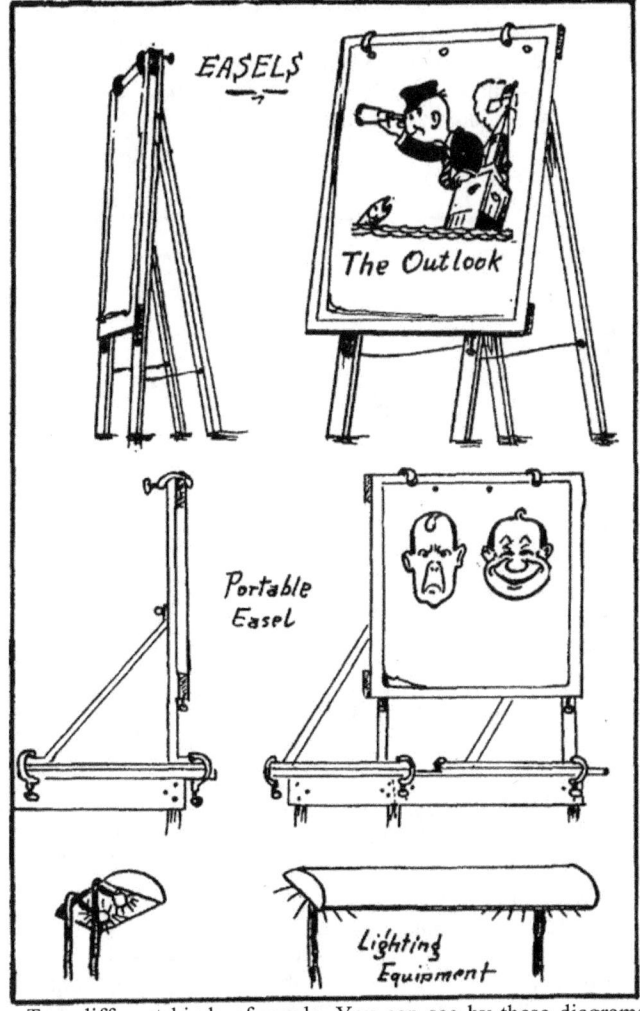

Two different kinds of easels. You can see by these diagrams how they are constructed. Both of these are the portable kind, and are constructed for convenience. The sketches below show a special lighting attachment.

a few minutes and placed in the proper position before the audience, is what is employed by all the chalk talkers who appear in public. Nearly every person following this line of public work has an easel made to suit his own individual re-

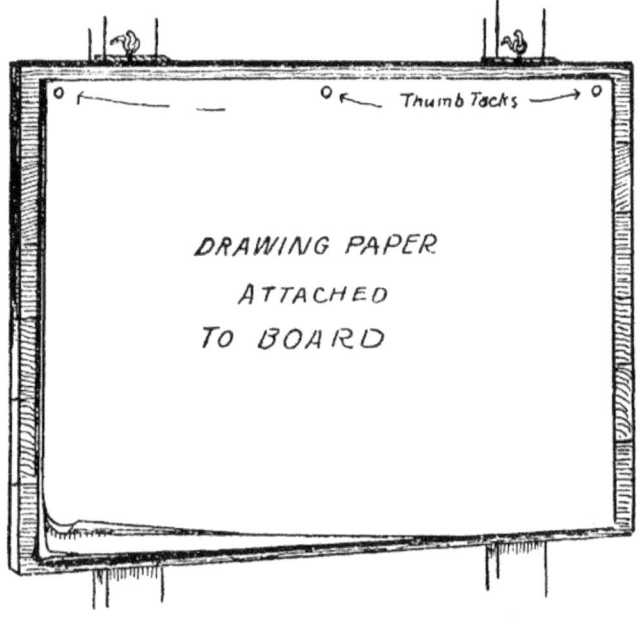

Thumb Tacks

DRAWING PAPER

ATTACHED

TO BOARD

A good board for a permanent place. Your crayon will work better if you keep several sheets of paper on the board all the time.

quirements. Diagrams of how these are made are shown on the accompanying pages.

Almost anything that is perfectly smooth will answer the purpose, if the paper can be firmly held down by thumbtacks or the kind of clamps used on quilting frames.

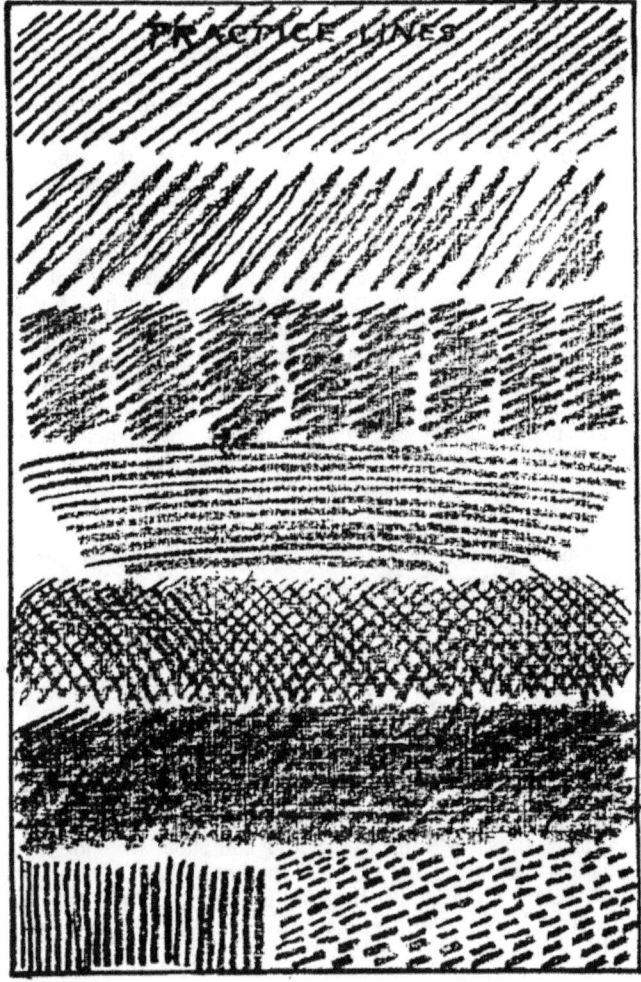

These practice sketches look simple and are simple, but they should be practiced until you are able to make uniform lines in any direction you wish.

If you have a blackboard available, use it to practice on, and even use it for demonstration purposes. Very good results may be obtained on a blackboard with colored crayons or chalk. The proper method of application is somewhat different than when white paper is used, yet the same results may be obtained. Whatever you use, whether blackboard or paper, it should be placed as nearly perpendicular as possible when you are working on it.

The advantage in having a board or easel that can be folded is the convenience in moving it from place to place. If you intend to use it regularly at one place, such as in your church, Sunday-school room, classroom, or home, the most convenient and economical board is one made of lumber or builders' board in such a way that it can be hung on the wall at a convenient height for use. Even if your board or wall space is a little uneven, the results on this account will be partially overcome by placing several sheets of paper on the board at a time, even though the top sheet is the only one then being used.

Usually, experienced chalk talkers use a rough-surfaced newsprint paper. Sheets are often fastened to the board at the top by means of ordinary quilting-frame clamps, and with large spring clips at the bottom. To remove sheets, the clip at lower left corner is loosened with the left hand, and with the right hand the sheet is seized and jerked upward with a free, swinging motion that breaks it from the fasteners at the top. A good practice to follow is to have ten or twenty sheets of paper on the board at a time. If clamps are not available to hold the paper in position, drive a few small nails through the top of the paper to hold it firmly to the easel. If you wish to preserve the drawings for someone in the audience, first loosen the clamp which holds the sheets at the bottom and carefully pull the sheet from the nails that hold it at the top, then drop it on the floor behind you. In nearly every .case there is someone who will want the drawings.

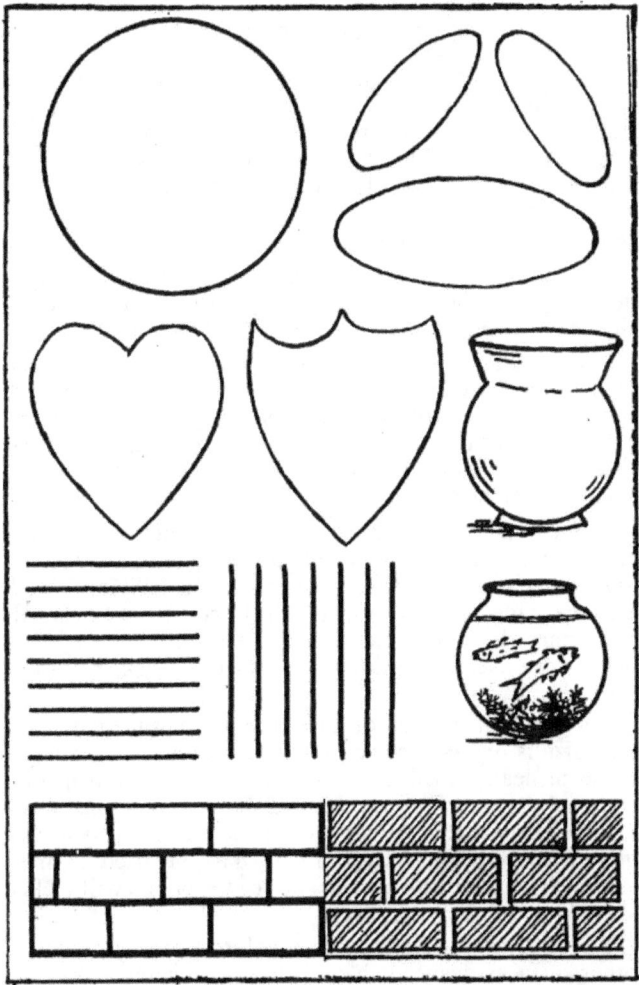

Practice making circles with a pencil. Start at the bottom and move to the left; then up and around to the starting point. Follow the same movement with the chalk, and draw ovals the same way as circles. In making large hearts, shields, and objects where both sides are uniform, use a piece of chalk in each hand and move both hands at the same time. This is good practice. It is well to practice straight lines a great deal.

CRAYONS AND COLOR

For many years the blackboard was largely used by speakers, and is thus employed to a large extent today; but the crayon and paper have proved to be better, and are now almost universally employed by people who have anything to do along the line of chalk talking. The white paper makes a good background for any color of crayon, and the audience is served better than they could possibly be by the blackboard.

In using paper for illustrating, one has no waste of time in erasing, for the used sheet of paper can be loosened and passed back over the top, where it is out of the way.

It *is* also an advantage to the artist when he wishes to produce a picture that will show upside down as well as right side up; the sheets of paper may be taken off the board and held in any position desired. Since the light background yields to different types and classes of illustration, paper has many decided advantages over the blackboard.

Ordinary newsprint paper, such as all printing offices carry, and on which their newspapers are printed, is the best and most economical. The size depends on your individual needs. Certain grades of book paper will do equally well, but the paper must have a mat or eggshell finish, for glossy book papers are useless. Ordinary newspaper stock *is* the best for practice work.

Lecturers' crayons are of different sizes, but the most practical size is one inch square by three inches long. These are made in nearly all the colors and can be secured in most stationery stores. They are nothing more than colored chalk, but the size of each piece permits it to be used in many ways to get different results. The corners may be used to make narrow lines, and with the flat surface the colors will yield to shading and tinting purposes.

An effective way of blending colors for backgrounds or other surfaces desiring shade is to use a chamois skin or a

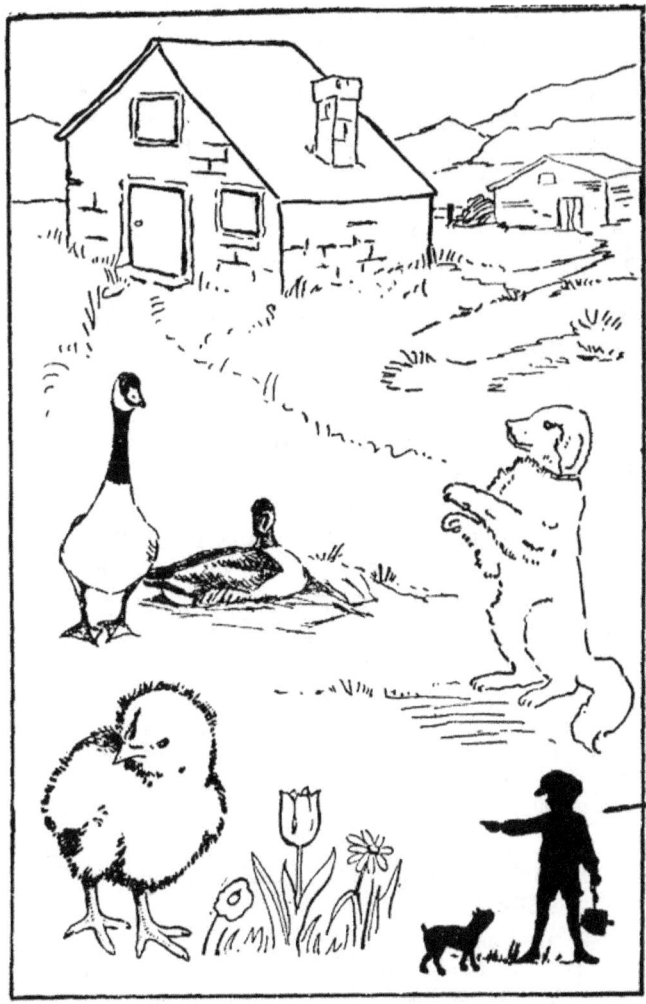

These are good sketches to practice on, either with pencil, pen, or chalk. Draw essential lines only—the fewer the better—to convey the idea. Make the houses first, then the other sketches. You will convince yourself that it is not half so hard as you thought it was. Draw each picture several times. It will help you to draw the next one better.

bunch of good cotton. After the chalk has been applied to the chamois or cotton it can easily be rubbed on the paper. There is no end to the possibilities of blending colors in this manner. A very light tint of any color may be obtained by applying a small amount of chalk and rubbing it well into the paper. A circular motion should be used in order to insure a uniform shade.

Yellow, red, and blue are called the primary colors. With the addition of white and black, every color and shade may be made from these by properly mixing. The primary colors or shades must be true to nature; they are then called ortho-chromatic, because the mixture will yield perfect tones.

Orange, violet, and green are the secondary colors, for blue mixed with yellow makes green; red and blue make violet; red and yellow make orange. Brown, gray, tan, and the count-less other shades are a mixture of different colors.

Red and yellow are called warm colors; also orange, which is the result of mixing these two colors. Red is the warmest color. Green and violet are cold colors, but blue is the coldest.

If a picture is to have distance, *it* is well to bear in mind that the warm colors suggest nearness, or the foreground, and the cold shades give distance.

Where sunlight is indicated, the coloring must be warm; although there may be green foliage, it may have the yellow shades predominating, and in shadow the colder colors should be more pronounced. The seasons of the year have their predominating colors which give them their peculiar settings.

The colors of spring are light blue sky, pale, yellow-green foliage, and the colors of twigs, limbs, and trunks of trees show red, purple, and brown.

In summer the sky is not such a deep blue, yellows are more prominent, the foliage greens are deeper, and more dark blues are used to deepen the shadows. Prussian blue is the base of

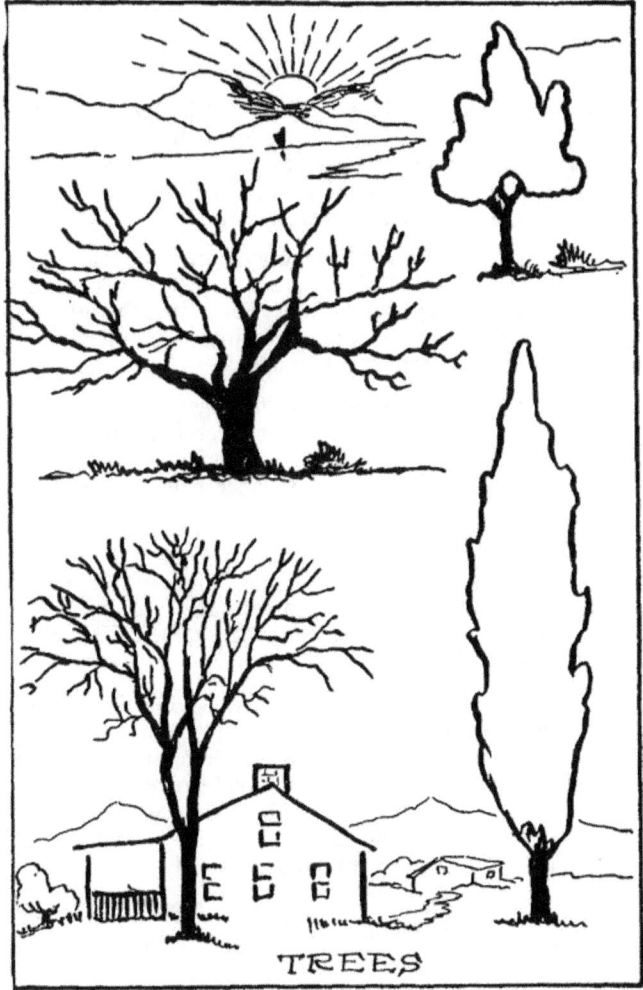

TREES

See the different kinds of trees and how they are made. Each represents a different type of tree. Try to make your copy as near like the picture in the book as you can. If you do not get it quite right, try it again. When you get so that you can make these well with the pencil, you will have no difficulty with your chalk or crayon.

greens, and ultramarine blue is the base of grays. This must be borne in mind when mixing to get some particular shade.

In autumn the sky is a hazy blue with tinges of yellow and purple. Greens in foliage are inclined toward olive. The browns and ocher predominate, and the frost turns the foliage to gold, orange, yellow, and red; but the bright colors in nature are short-lived and change rapidly.

In winter the sky is light gray, with deeper grays in distances. Browns and blacks are in evidence, and the snow gives blue and purplish shadows. For hazy days, gray must be used to soften the colors of the whole picture; for rainy days, a bluish tint must be in evidence.

In using colored chalk in your drawings, the effect is sometimes disappointing when viewed under artificial light. Yellows tend to disappear or show as white. Orange is often substituted for yellow at an evening performance when white paper is used.

A good way to test colors under artificial light is to view your drawing from the rear of the building and see v/hat happens to your colored drawings on the stage or platform. Colors viewed in daylight often appear quite different un-'er other kinds of illumination.

For the best effect, the chalk talker should strive for strong contrasts and bright colors. Strong high lights and shadows are what please the average audience. For instance, a moonlight scene, in which the shadows are broad strokes of black, will make a pleasing impression on the audience when the artist finishes his picture with yellow high lights of ripples on the water and lights shining from windows.

When subdued outlines are desired, a good-sized wad of cotton will help to blend the colors.

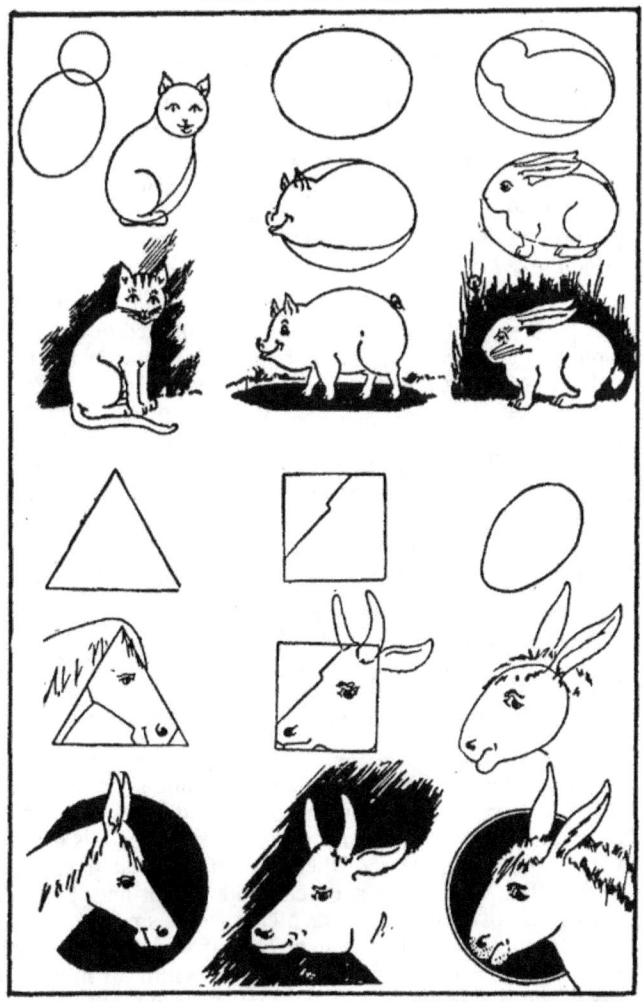

Sketches after Cobb Shinn.

Now, with your pencil in hand, you can make a cat from a double circle—perhaps not as good as the picture above at first, but if you try a few times you can. Then from the oval make the pig and bunny. The triangle, square, and oval look more difficult, but try them and see how easy they are.

HINTS FOR BEGINNERS

It is always interesting to watch different individuals in an audience when a chalk drawing is being made. The thing that interests them is that they do not know what is going to be made, and it is a good plan to foster that curiosity. The chalk talker should stand aside occasionally as if to scrutinize the picture, but with the main object of giving the audience a good look.

Any drawing should be practiced several times with pencil and paper or with the crayon before it is offered to the public. Until you get used to appearing before the public, or if ydu are not sure of being able to produce the picture in a satisfactory manner, carefully trace the picture with a pencil beforehand. Light pencil lines may be seen by yourself but not by your audience. The heavy lines of your crayon may be placed directly over the pencil marks, and you will be able to make better speed, as well as draw the picture more perfectly. The crayon drawing should always be made with plain, distinct strokes, and only lines that mean something should be made.

Remember, one is not required to be an artist in order to use the material in this book effectively and profitably. The amateur has been kept in mind constantly. The name of the book itself is intended to convey the idea that anyone with ordinary intelligence can apply these methods with profit and satisfaction.

The best way to begin is to try to imitate some picture in this book or some face or object pictured elsewhere. Try to duplicate every line as nearly as possible, for there is a reason why every mark is placed where it is. If you wish to enlarge a picture, first with a rule and pencil draw light lines each way across it, covering the entire picture with small squares of equal size—say one-fourth inch. Then if you want to increase your drawing three times in height or width, or nine times the size of the original, rule your paper in the same manner as your picture, only with squares three-fourths inch instead on one-fourth. (See diagram below.)

By carefully noting the position of each square you can reproduce the copy in the larger form with considerable degree

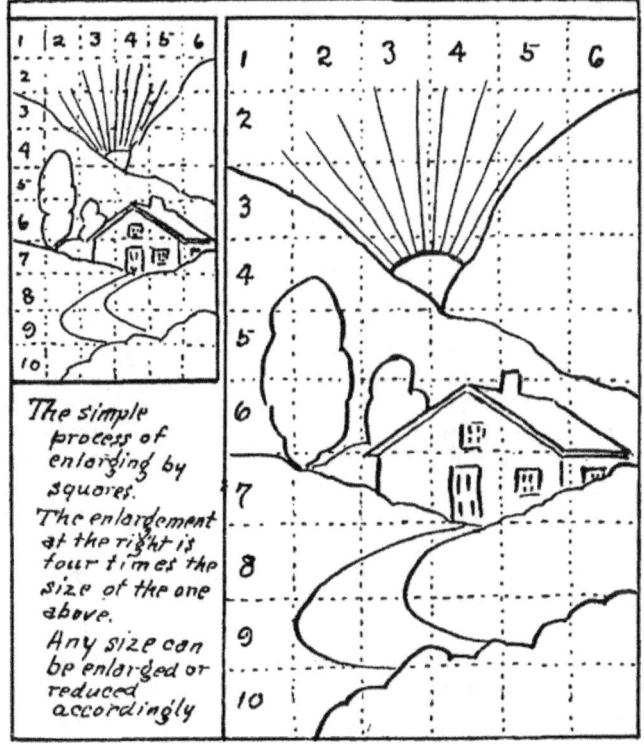

You can enlarge any picture to any size by the method pictures above. It is by this method that the large billboards are painted. Read the text for full explanation—page 32,

of accuracy. Practice copying pictures, diagrams, and letters of the alphabet until you become familiar with making your lines where you want them. Then try copying offhand—without guide lines. Make good enlarged copies of the pictures and sketches in this book as you go along.

When you have practiced sufficiently so you can draw your objects, then you should put into your drawings some of your own ideas and be original.

Still use the ideas pictured in this book and apply and adapt them to your own work. You will soon find by applying thoughts that come to you while working that you have something just as original and practical as the figures and illustrations in this book. Apply ideas and illustrations from almost every known source, taking them from a thought here and a suggestion there, and in the finished product they will become your own.

Much depends on constant practice if you would succeed in chalk talk as a teacher, Sunday-school worker, young people's leader, or an entertainer; yet by practicing the lessons and drawing over and over the characters in this book, or the pictures you adapt from various sources, you will become so apt that you can adapt any new thought in your own easy manner.

I have heard people say, "I just cannot draw; why, I couldn't draw a straight line." It is not necessary to draw a straight line when you begin, but *it is* necessary to have an earnest desire to succeed, or you will not progress very far in any line of endeavor.

When a person decides, "I am going to succeed" in this or that, and persistently continues to apply himself, the battle is the same as won—the rest is easy.

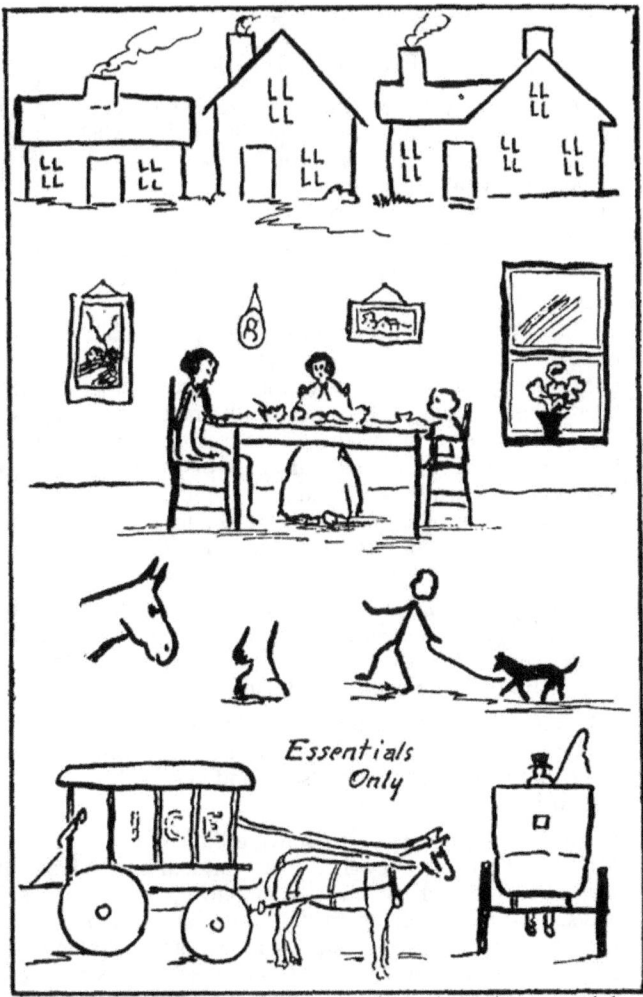

Essentials
Only

Watch carefully how the lines are made on these pictures, and draw your pencil sketches as near like the copy as you can. Practice makes perfect. The second attempt will be easier and the results better than the first.

LEARNING TO DRAW

The only way to learn how to draw is by drawing, and then by drawing some more. Begin by deciding what you want to make; then try to make your marks with a whole-arm movement in full, free lines, avoiding the making of sketchy lines or strokes with no purpose in view.

Practice making your strokes firmly; hold the crayon between the thumb and first two fingers, so that you can control your every move.

With everything in readiness, your paper held firmly in place and your crayon ready, begin your practice of horizontal lines. Stand nearly at arm's length from your paper or blackboard. Start making a horizontal chalk line at a point opposite the left shoulder; throw the weight of the body on the left foot; and, placing the piece of chalk on the board, keeping the wrist and arm fairly rigid, draw your chalk toward the right by swaying the body until the weight rests on the right foot. Practice this movement repeatedly, until you can make straight lines to suit you.

To draw vertical lines, start at a point opposite the right shoulder and about as high as the top of your head; use the whole-arm movement, bearing down firmly, and come downward with uniform speed to the end of the stroke.

Practice these lines again and again; you will soon see that the technique of making straight lines consists almost wholly in getting control of your muscles and nerves. Practice alone will enable you to succeed.

You should also practice drawing circles. Face the blackboard, stand close enough to that you can easily reach the surface with the chalk at arm's length—up, down, and sideways. You should stand firmly and with the shoulder in a fixed position; swing the stiff arm around and keep the crayon on the surface of the paper or board. Practice this movement until you can make a fairly accurate circle. In making a small

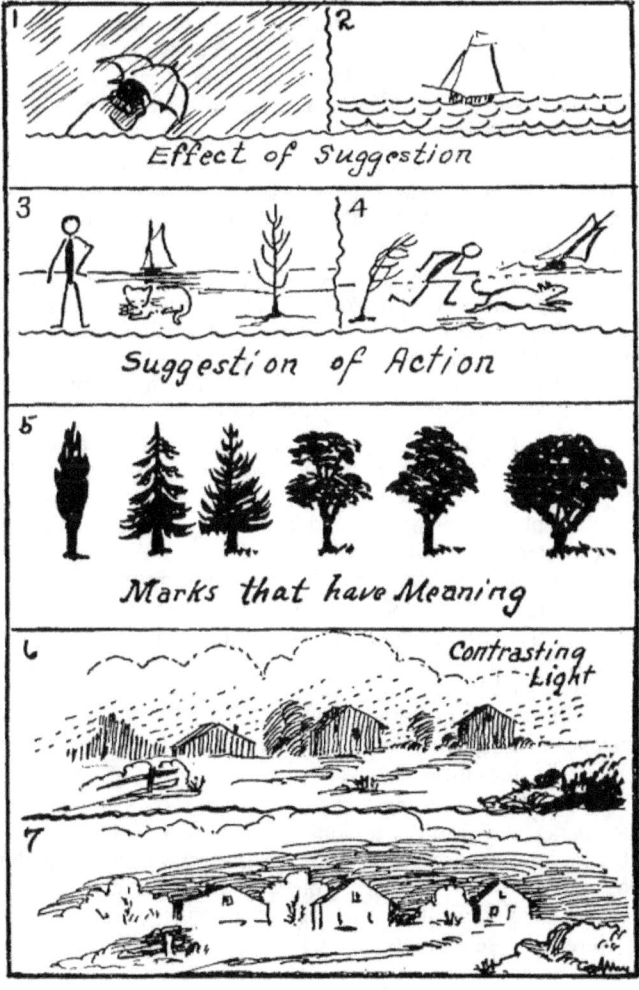

1. The slanting marks suggest rain when the umbrella is seen. 2. So the simple marks suggest water with the sailboat. 3 and 4. Inaction and action. 6 and 7. Different effects caused by sources of light.

circle, start at the bottom and move the chalk to the left, then up and around to starting point. You should practice circles and straight lines until you can make them confidently, accurately, and quickly. Daily practice of five minutes will bring marvelous results.

A drawing, even though it be somewhat inaccurate, will hold the attention of the audience or class and be more satisfactory if it is made freely, rapidly, and accurately, than if made in a doubtful movement.

It is not the intention of this book to go into the principles of drawing, such as the horizon line, ground line, point of sight, vision line, perspective, vanishing point, observation point, and shading. However, a general knowledge of all these must be obtained before one can enter into the making of pictures that may truly be classed as works of art.

In another chapter the principles of perspective are given briefly. Each picture, even the crudest sketch, must incorporate some of these principles, to look at all right. When the elementary steps of design and drawing in this book have been mastered, the worker who is interested will take up the subject further in order to master these principles.

A few marks with a pencil or crayon, put in the right place, immediately *give* the appearance of distance; but it is necessary to know how to make the right marks and lines to accomplish this. By carefully noticing the various sketches in this book you will readily understand what this means. Observe the sketches and drawings in almost any publication and see how simply the lines make the picture.

Whenever you see simple sketches, try to copy them, making the marks as nearly as possible like the original. By close observation you can see why the marks have been given the positions they occupy, and you will almost unconsciously acquire much definite knowledge of drawing and design.

Here are a few points that will help you in planning your pictures:

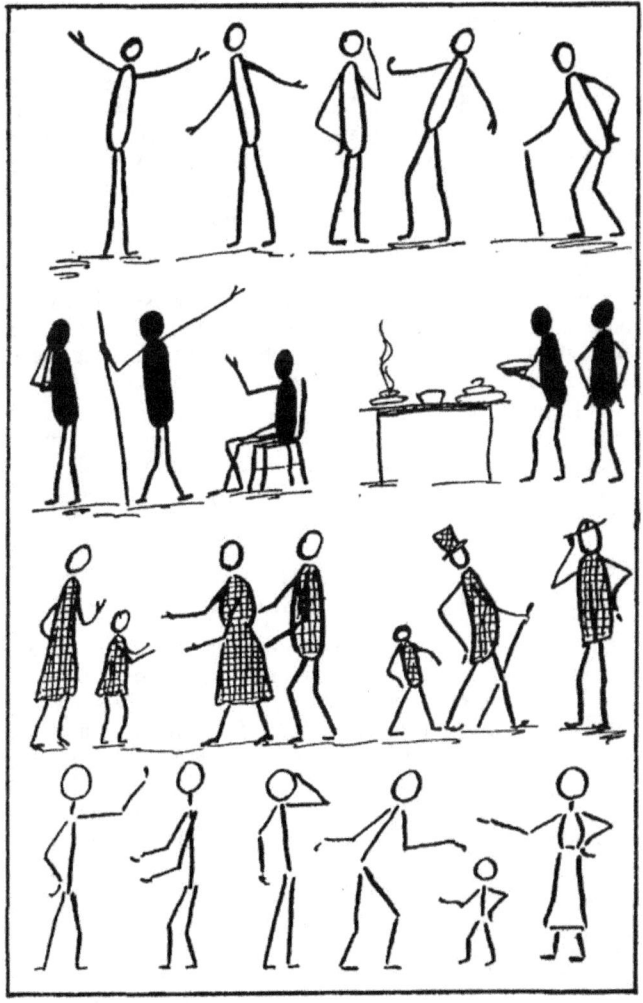

These figures are used as the simplest way of representing human figures. A great deal of expression may be had from such figures. These are very easy to make. Take your pencil, pen, or chalk and try these figures—starting at the top row. Try every one all the way down. See page 19 also.

A panel picture, whether upright or horizontal, is generally more pleasing than a square one.

There is a center of interest in every well-composed picture, whether it be of a human figure, a group of animals, a cabin, boat, windmill, mountain peak, waterfall, road or tree; and this center of interest should never be in the exact center of the picture. Some artists prefer it above the center and to one side—preferably the upper left, as the theory is advanced that the eye first falls there from the habit of looking there when beginning to read a page.

This center of interest need not be the largest object in the picture, but its color or the leading lines should draw attention to it. Often a boat is the center of interest in a water picture, or some clouds in the sky may help to make a perfect balance.

A figure in action always attracts attention; even a few flying birds in the sky add interest, but these should not be placed mechanically—that is, not two or three in a straight line. Three birds are better than two, or any odd number better than an even.

HOW TO BEGIN

At this point in your own individual life you may never have tried to do much with crayon or chalk. You may be at a loss just how to get started and where to begin. The simple fact that you are reading *Chalk Talk Made Easy* proves your interest in the subject; and where there is interest, there may be developed an ability to succeed in this work. It is now up to you to obtain your training by following a plan you may map out for yourself, to fit your own individual case and circumstances in life.

"But just where shall I begin?" you ask. In the first place, the great essential is the proper equipment. It may be ever so meager and limited in the various articles eventually needed, but what you *get* should be of the best. Poor materials and

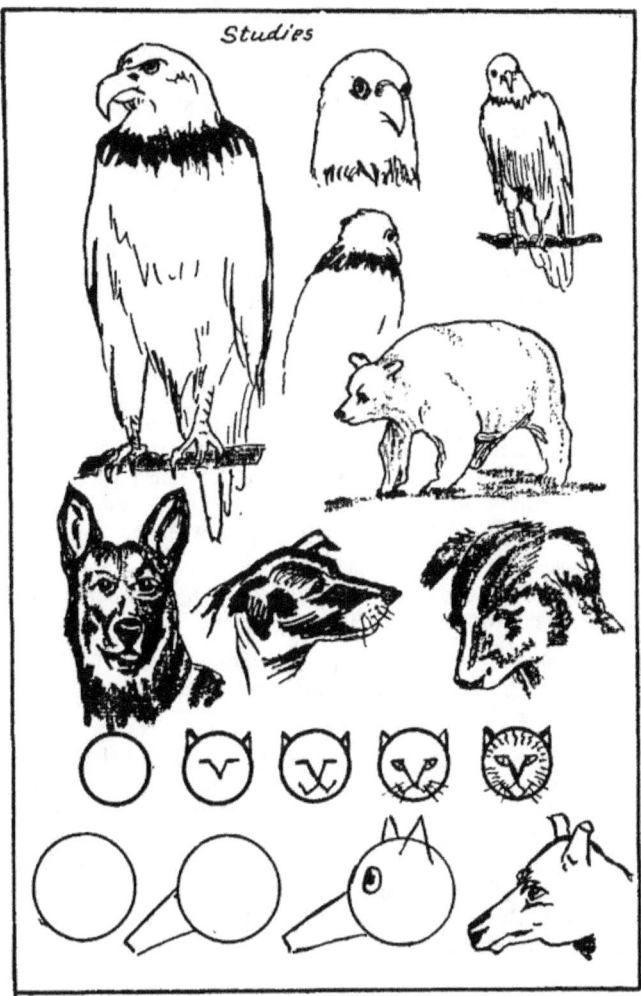

Studies

Good practice bird and animal studies. It is well to be able to draw these studies, as they will come in handy someday. The circles are always interesting.

equipment will have a tendency to handicap you in the beginning, and this alone may discourage you. A determination to succeed, even against all obstacles, will surmount a lack of proper necessities.

A drawing board or easel must be provided according to one of the plans given in the chapter on "How to Make a Drawing Board." Then get a good assortment of lecturer's crayons—size 1x3 inches, a yardstick, and a soft cloth. The cloth is very useful in wiping the hands when soiled with the crayon. Many chalk talkers have a thin slip-on coat or a painter's smock, for the protection of their clothing while using the chalk.

Gloves tend to destroy a person's sense of touch, so are used by very few artists. When working with the bare chalk, it is wise to prepare by putting talcum powder on the hands in advance. This aids in removal of chalk from the hands with soap afterwards. Some artists use cold cream on their hands before starting, and then use more cold cream in removing chalk from the hands. A final cleanup is made with soap and water.

Always put a sheet of paper on the floor if you are working in a home or where there *is* a carpet or rugs, for chalk dust is hard to remove from carpets.

It has been said that any person should be able to do good work with good tools and equipment, but it takes an artist to do good work with poor tools.

Get a good supply of paper from a newspaper shop, so that you can fill hundreds of sheets with just practice marks of jets, daffodils, moon faces, smiles, frowns, noses, eyes, ears, hands, feet, dogs, cats, trees, houses, and everything else illustrated in this book. That is why the pictures were put in this book—for your practice. There are none that are too difficult. By trying the easiest and simplest first and then going step by step, the drawings and stunts are easy and can be mastered if you but try. There is not an object pictured

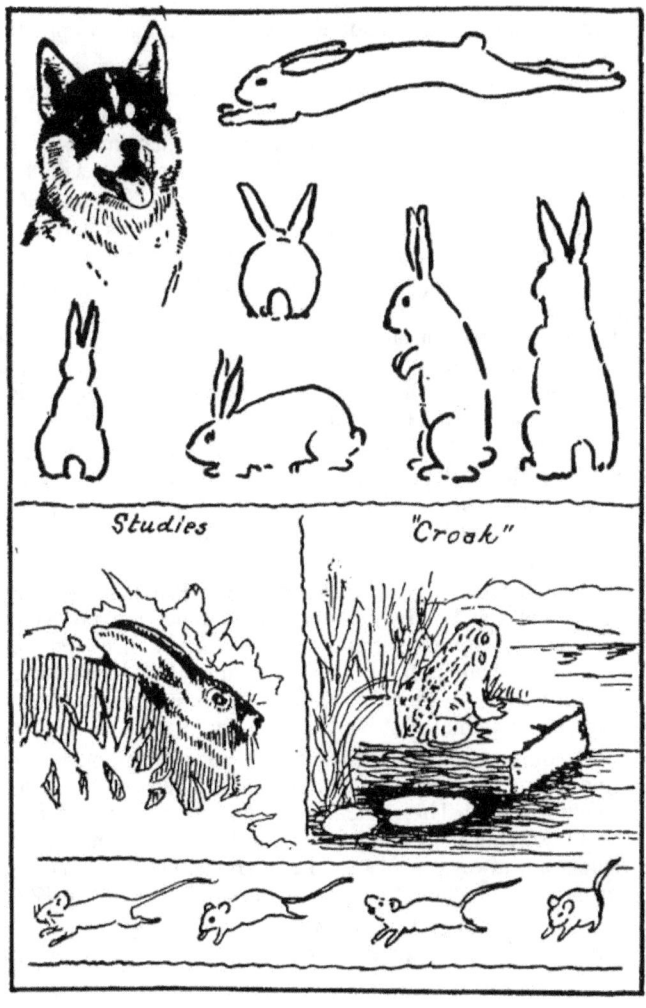

Some good animal poses. It is well to know how to draw all of these. It will help you in drawing more difficult objects.

here but can be used at some time to advantage. So practice all of them.

If in years to come you have mastered the principles in this book and are numbered among America's chalk artists, and you can look back upon this book as the starting point or as a steppingstone to success, this little volume will have accomplished its mission and I shall be repaid for its preparation.

"What can I get out of this book on chalk talk and blackboard drawing?" should be the big question in your mind. The answer will depend altogether on how you apply the book to yourself and yourself to the book. You can get a great deal of satisfaction and pleasure to yourself, and you can start out in public demonstration after a little practice, by using some of the suggestions and adapting new applications until you have selected your own individual program.

This book will help you find yourself. You will soon decide for yourself which pictures are practical by the way they appeal to the public. In personal presentation you will develop some individual characteristics that will be your very own. Everyone does this.

In the chapter, "How to Prepare Your Program," are many suggestions, and you will soon be able to adapt many pictures and subjects to your various needs. Make use of the enlarging process in chapter on "Hints for Beginners," and the tracing of the drawings explained in the same chapter on all your sketches which at first may seem difficult.

If you want a religious or temperance program, you will find it here. Several programs may be built around the chapter, "Symbols and Their Meaning," and also "Crayon in the Sunday School." Some of the simple surprise and turnover stunts are always in place. They may be used in almost any program and adapted to suit the occasion. (See page 127.)

Chalk talk is and always will be something that holds the interest of almost any kind of audience. The interest lies

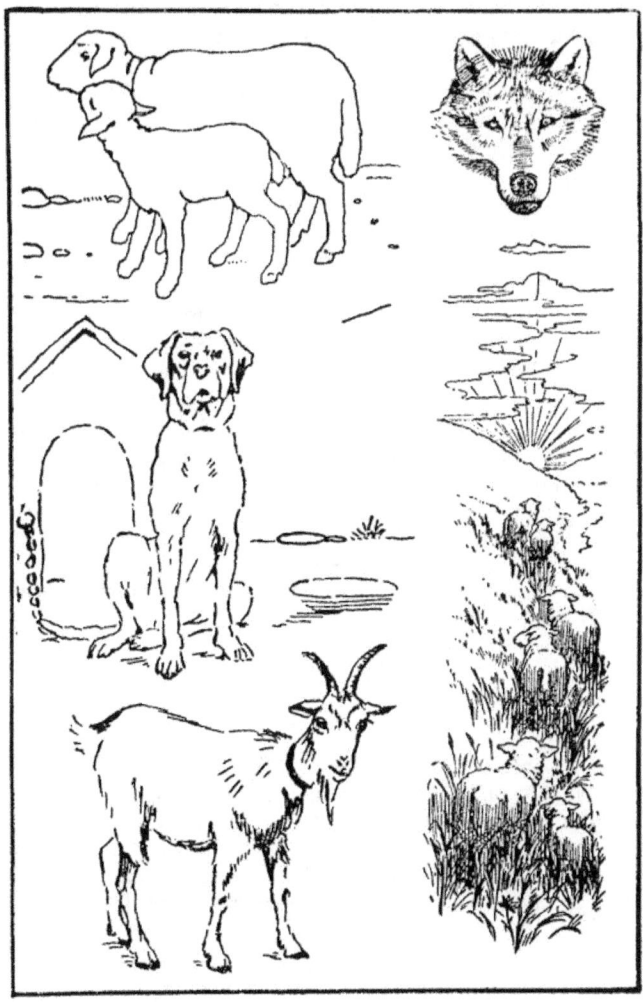

More animal studies—not a hard subject in the lot.

in the fact that the spectator *is* kept in anticipation of what the next move will bring.

Your first attempts at chalk talk may be crude, but by using a number of the stunts in this book you will find it interesting; and experience will develop your capabilities.

What you need is the experience of making some of the simplest drawings before such friendly audiences as await you in your own community. You should get your preparatory experience before church, school, and social organizations made up of people you know the best and who are interested in you. This is the only way to learn. You will expand naturally. Your field is as large as you make it. The first and most important step is to make a beginning—now.

Before you close this book make up your mind to start at once. Get your materials as soon as possible and begin—not next week, but at once—at least plan now and prepare at the earliest possible moment. The book in your hand is full of gold nuggets and is worth a great deal to you. Whether you are a blacksmith, farmer, factory worker, clerk, stenographer, day laborer, teacher, preacher—man or woman—boy or girl— in whatever pursuit, *Chalk Talk Made Easy* is an open door of opportunity for your future.

YOU CAN DO IT

To be able to do freehand drawing on a blackboard or with crayons on paper should interest every teacher or speaker in public, whether his message is religious, educational, or social. The ability to use chalk talk in making a point clear, or to impress a lesson on the audience, is invaluable. One speaker said: "A piece of chalk is worth more than a lot of talk."

Many teachers and speakers would like to use illustrations in connection with their messages, but they do not know where

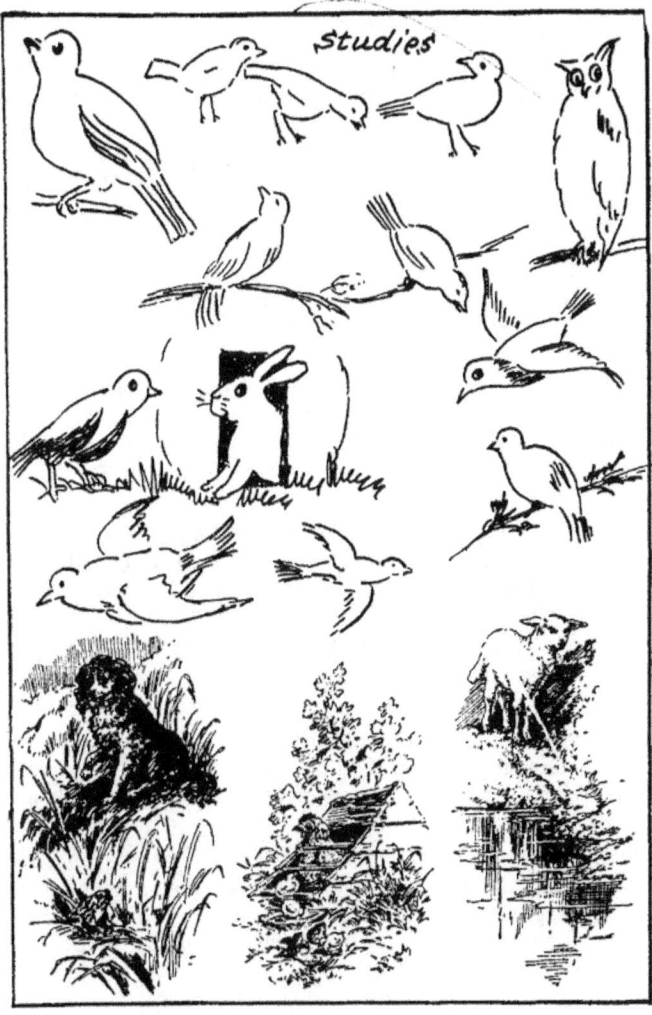

Bird studies may be used in many ways. Many different kinds of birds are mentioned in the Bible. Adapt some of these sketches to Bible lessons.

to begin—the whole thing seems a great big something that only "natural-born artists" should tackle; but if the truth were known, "natural-born artists" are few and far between. The ability of a practical chalk talker comes only by having an intense desire to do it, a willingness to start, a determination to accomplish it, and a doggedness to overcome obstacles. In fact, it takes that much to succeed in any line of endeavor. But if a person once starts to draw, he will find every step an easy one and full of interest.

In this book there are many simple sketches intended to aid by giving suggestions and by furnishing the necessary principles that will enable any person with ordinary ability to draw for pleasure or profit.

Many persons have neither the time nor inclination to take up a complete course in drawing, as most courses cover so many phases of the subject that the information and knowledge wanted would not justify such a great expenditure of time and money.

This book is not a complete treatise on the subject of drawing or art; but if any person will take the time to study and put in practice the information herein given, he can make a success insofar as he applies his natural ability and adaptability.

The important step is to begin now. All who will apply themselves will find a pathway lined with interest, pleasure, and real usefulness.

The writer has especially seen the need of chalk and crayon in connection with Sunday-school and young people's work, since there are so many ways of applying diagrams, illustrations, and the like to every lesson. There is nothing like a crayon drawing to impress a point in the lesson to the class.

In connection with Sunday-school work, with a little practice the average teacher can develop and make use of chalk drawings with results decidedly beneficial, both to the teacher and

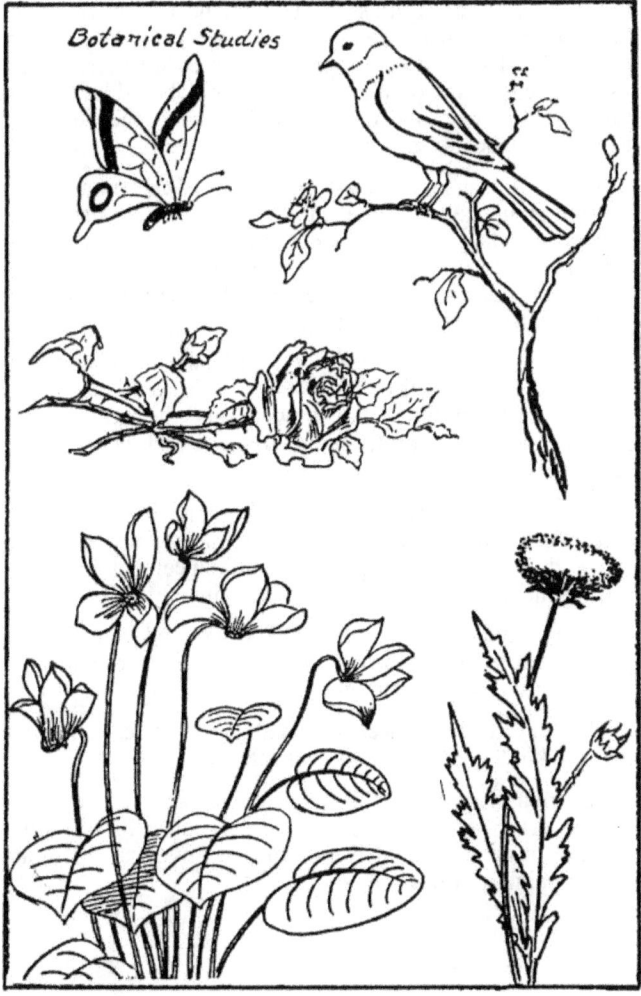

Botanical Studies

By using different colors of chalk you can make pictures of flowers in colors, which are greatly needed to add variety to your chalk talk. In Christ's parables he often mentioned flowers of the field.

the class. Too much stress should not be put on the chalk drawings, as they may be employed so freely that they become formal; the chalk should be used only for a direct and distinct result. The truths and points of the lesson should be brought out in such a way that the drawing clinches the point and brings home the message.

If a drawing should be made so very, very clever and artistic that the audience would be impressed mainly by its beauty, very little lasting benefit would result—it would merely have furnished entertainment. But if the drawing impresses the truth upon the minds of the hearers, the chalk-talk drawing will have accomplished its purpose.

To learn the use of the crayon will take more work and persistence for some than for others; but the better acquainted one is with the rudiments of drawing, and the more practice one has, the more confidence he will have and the better will be the results.

When interest takes hold of any person, practice will result. When practice brings one to the place where he knows he can do it, that knowledge gives confidence; and confidence is of prime importance to anyone appearing before the public.

If you have a desire to do chalk work (and you no doubt have, or you would not be reading this book), you can do it— if your desire is strong enough.

The student's final success depends on practice, ability, and interest; but the greatest of these is interest.

Too great haste to reap the fruit of success, even before the seed of practice has been sown and the plant cultivated, will be fatal to advancement in this line of endeavor, as in any other business of life.

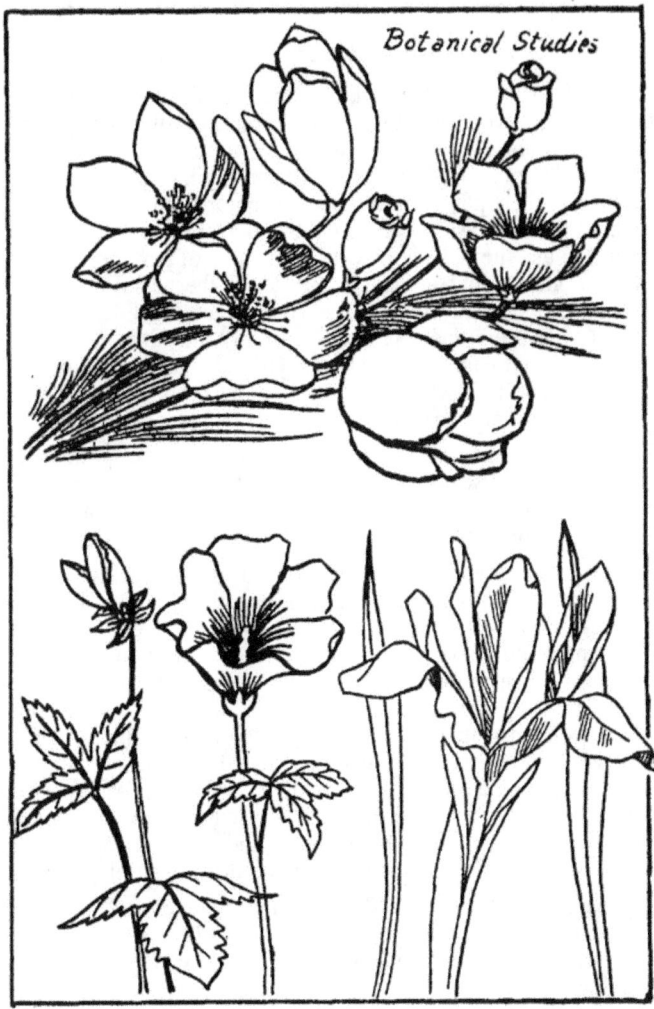

Botanical Studies

By using your colored chalk your pictures of flowers need not lack variety. Use a darker shade or the same color where shadows are needed, on both leaves and flowers.

HOW TO PREPARE YOUR PROGRAM

If you wish to produce quite a difficult picture before your audience, take your time to sketch it carefully with a lead pencil in light lines at home. Follow the instructions given in chapter, "Hints for Beginners," on enlarging by the use of squares. When pencil drawings are completed, arrange the sheets on your easel in the rotation and order in which you intend to use them, but place a clean sheet of paper on top so that no one in your audience will detect the pencil sketches. When you get ready to produce your picture—while you are giving your preliminary remarks, casually turn this sheet over the top of your easel, or pull it off. This can easily be done, as the clamps or nails which hold your sheets to the board should be used across the top only.

The pencil lines will act as a guide to you. Take your time and carefully draw each line or mark with your crayon without anyone in your audience being the wiser, for these faint lines will not be visible to them.

This plan is a good one for a beginner to follow while learning, for it gives confidence and will be a great help in putting on the first few programs. Make your crayon lines firm and quite heavy. Even with black crayon the marks will not be too heavy for the most distant eyes in your audience. Keep a steady nerve. Draw your lines slowly and well, but with decision, pausing now and then to make some remark; and while doing so, step aside so that the audience can see what you are doing. The sketching process may be used advantageously in any program. It will enable you to demonstrate much more speed before your audience, since no great amount of time will be required for thinking out details.

The patience of an audience should never be taxed on account of long, drawn-out pictures. Simple lines—each having a place and meaning—are what will make you successful in chalk talk.

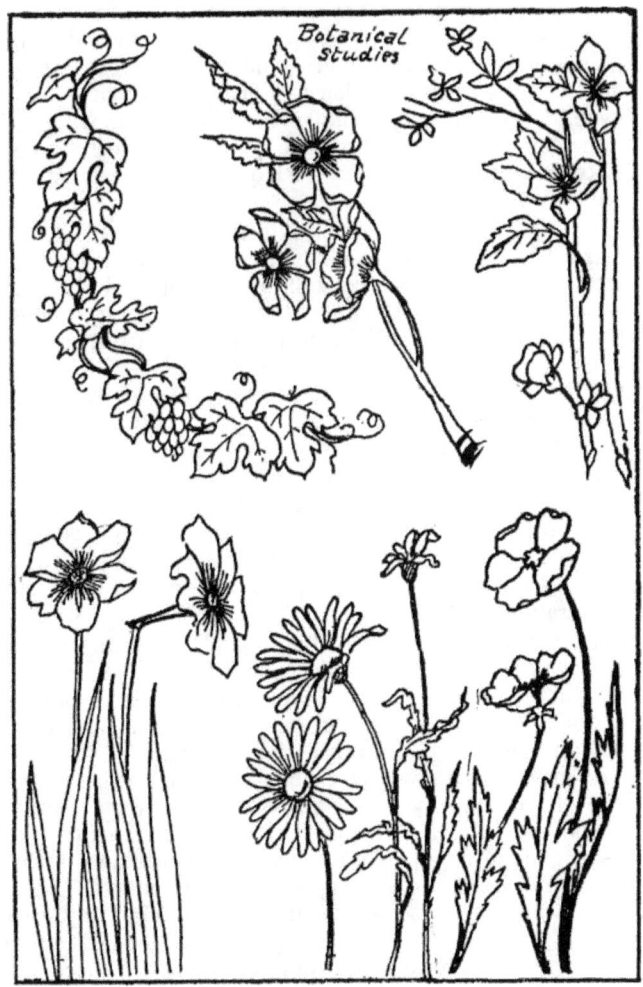

Botanical studies

Practice making these flowers. They are easy to make and often such pictures are needed. Their practice is beneficial.

Preparedness is another great essential if you would become a successful chalk talker. You should practice on each drawing until you become so familiar with its formation that you can eventually be looking in another direction and drawing at the same time. Don't think you can become a successful chalk talker in a few hours, or a day—it requires practice, the same as any other line of art.

Possibly you have more talent to chalk than to talk, or vice versa. The artist who is qualified to do both well is the fellow who is usually most successful; however, many artists never speak a word. It is left entirely to the individual to overcome his shortcomings, and he can qualify as a first-class chalk talker if he is sincere and earnest in his endeavor. The writer has in mind a clever chalk talker who talks incessantly—so much so that the audience tires of it. They want to see what he is doing more than they want to hear what he has to say, especially when the talk is just "talk."

It is necessary that you put earnest study and practice into your work. It would be foolish to attempt complete chalk-talk programs or platform work unless you feel capable of making good. This confidence comes by careful preparation.

Do not be hasty in attempting a public performance; wait until you possess self-confidence and feel assured of a successful undertaking. Practice your program in the presence of your home folks or friends—this will give you confidence—then appear before clubs or social gatherings or your class. You may or may not have experienced being before an audience. If you have, you will find it a great advantage in your chalk-talk work; but if you have not—there is no need of having stage fright, if you keep your nerve and think of what you are doing and saying. Just "be yourself"; or, in other words, show some individuality and originality. By so doing, you will make a better impression on the audience and consequently help to make your performance a success. Do not try to see how fast you can talk and chalk. Speed will develop with practice. Make it a point to speak fluently. Give

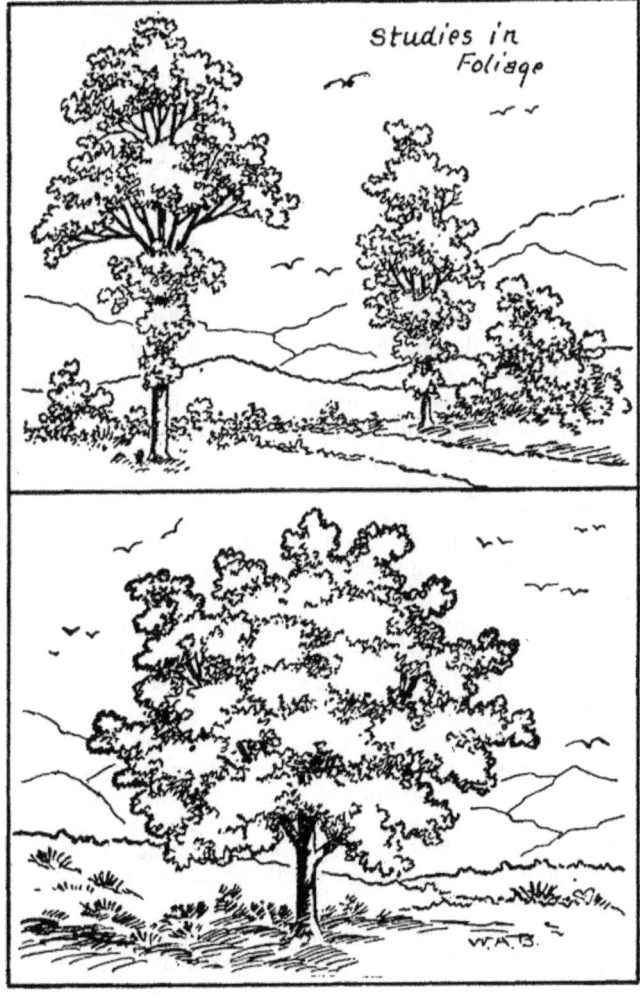

Studies in foliage. Note carefully how the high lights and shadows are made. The high lights are the white paper. Too many marks spoil the simplicity of the picture.

the audience time to comprehend what you say and do. Take your time, so you will not lose self-control or get confused.

Crudeness of execution will be forgiven by the audience if there is a definite plan, or point, or plot back of your picture. Snap and brevity are necessary in chalk-talk work. After successful attempts have been made, work calling for more skill should be tried. An audience will soon tire of mere drawing; but a wise chalk talker will produce some short, snappy, pointed sketches.

A trick, or surprise sketch, should be resorted to occasionally. A carefully made marine, landscape, portrait, or cartoon should not be put on during the first part of the program, but saved for near the end. Even then this should not be attempted until you have had practice sufficient to insure confidence in your execution; and part of this practice should be with the idea of concealing the final result, at least until the last few seconds before its completion.

If you can keep your audience guessing what the final result is going to be, their interest will become more intense. Likewise, if the nature of your sketch remains unknown until you reveal it to the audience as a crowning climax, they will be all the more highly pleased. Practice is of the greatest importance in success; so practice, practice, practice.

A "good-night stunt" is good to use in winding up your program. The safest way, as a rule, is to close with a note of good cheer.

In making your start in chalk talking, you will find an abundance of material in this book, both in suggestions and drawings, to start you out. Practice the sketches which appeal most to you. Make them over and over, until you can make them while only half thinking what you are doing; then start out. The best work possible should be thrown into the close of your program.

The successful chalk talker is always on the alert for new ideas. He trains himself to grasp ideas from daily happenings,

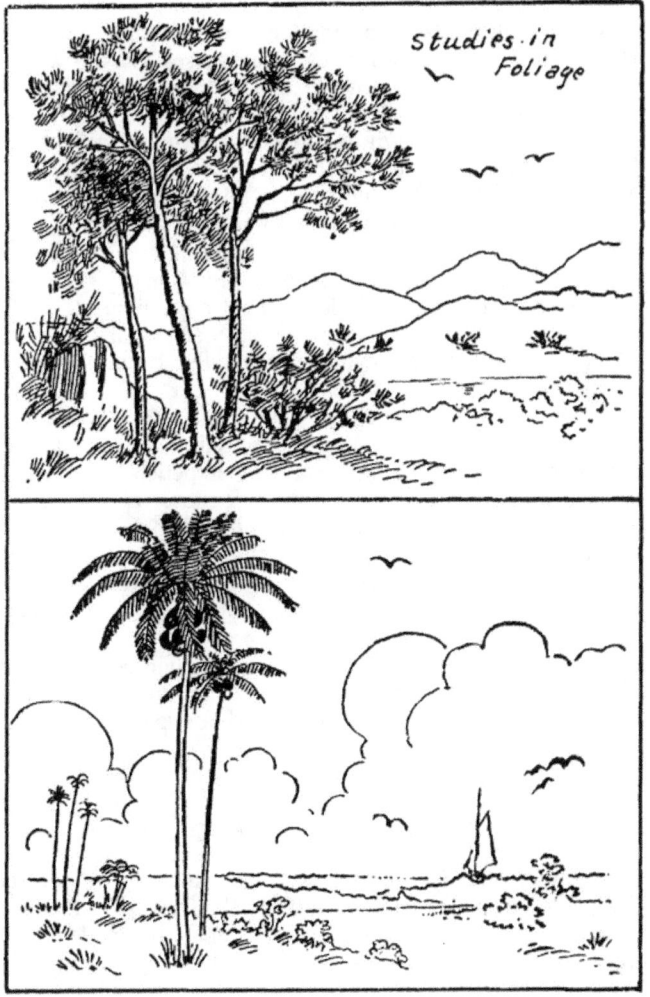

In tropical sketches use tropical trees. The lower picture is easily made and yields to a moonlight subject well. In case this is desired cover entire surface first with blue-gray chalk, blend with cotton, then use light yellow for moon and reflections on water and black for trees and landscape.

newspaper stories and cartoons, and the national holidays. He searches publications for new ideas, verses, etc. It is well to keep your programs seasonable. If you are scheduled to *give* a chalk talk on Labor Day, Lincoln's birthday, New Year's, or Christmas, work in drawings that are timely. When you happen into a town, try to learn what has been going on. Make the audience feel that you are interested in their town, and try to produce something that will interest them.

After you have practiced your programs until you can handle them with accuracy and freedom, break in by *giving* a performance at some local club, school entertainment, public meeting, young people's meeting, Sunday school, or luncheon. After a few performances you will naturally acquire the knack of entertaining.

Do not expect any great financial returns at first. When your work has earned you a reputation you will be in a position to set your own price for your services. Experience, even at a considerable cost of time and money, is more valuable to you than to receive pay for your services. However, do not refuse if someone wants to help you out in a financial way. One way of doing after you get started is to plan an entertainment and invite everybody; then let the audience contribute whatever they feel like giving.

You can make a success of this art if you will go into it with the determination to succeed. Just keep everlastingly at it, and eventually you will be rewarded for keeping up your courage.

A RECORD OF IDEAS AND COLOR

An item of great value to anyone who works along the lines of chalk talking or public illustrating is a small notebook in which rough sketches may be made of all posters or pictures one sees along the way or finds in

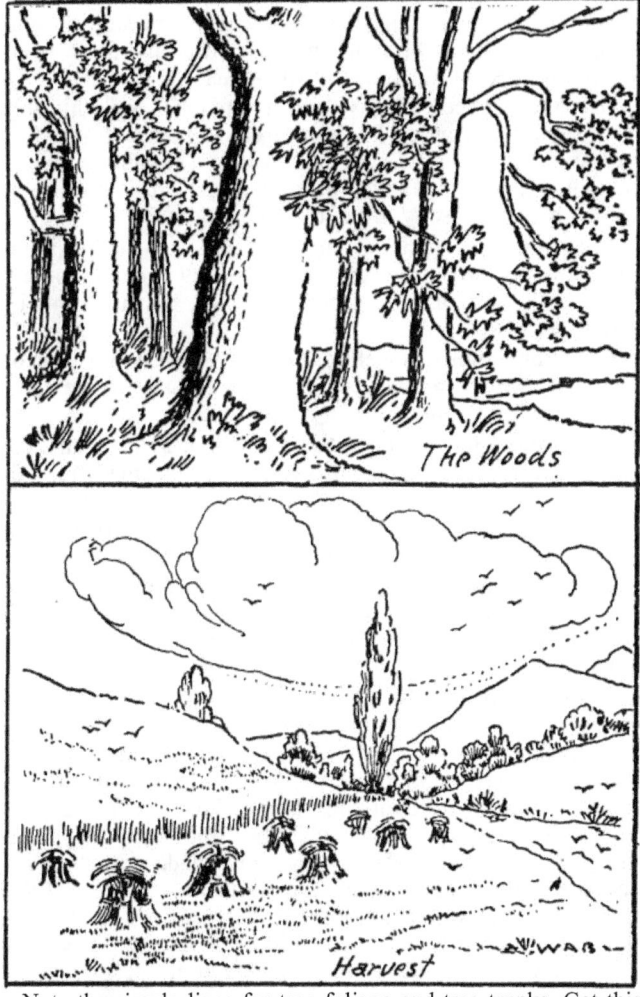

Note the simple lines for tree foliage and tree trunks. Get this point. The white paper forms the high lights in both upper and lower pictures.

books, magazines, or papers. Many splendid suggestions for illustrations may be found in places here and there, even when a person is not looking for ideas.

To make a success of any venture one must apply himself to the task; the more he is interested in his work, the greater the success he will have in it. Thought produces thought; many an idea will present itself and, if not jotted down, may slip away from the mind forever.

The author has gathered thoughts and ideas while riding along the road or in street cars, while sitting in church or at a public gathering, on a walk in the country, or while lying in bed at night.

In making notes it is well to jot down any original*idea or suggestion which presents itself at that time, or while the mind is dwelling on the incident.

Some of the modern advertising on billboards contains the very finest of bulletin art; also, the color schemes are well worthy of notice.

In making your sketches, a notation of colors used is helpful if you desire to use colored crayons in your design or are planning a poster for a special occasion.

You cannot use just any colors and put two of them side by side and produce a harmonious picture effect. The artist knows the harmony of color and uses the proper combinations to produce a pleasing effect. It is well to take note of pleasant color combinations and study them.

By observing the colors in nature you will find harmony. Most of Nature's colors are pleasing in their soft, mellow tones. The most brilliant sunsets are short-lived. The sun's rays which are responsible for the brilliant shades of yellow, orange, and red also cast a harmonious shade over the landscape till all is aglow with the beautiful harmony. Even shadows in the water harmonize; the sea, deep-blue under the rays of the noonday sun, loses its deep blues and greens, to a certain extent, while the sunset glow continues.

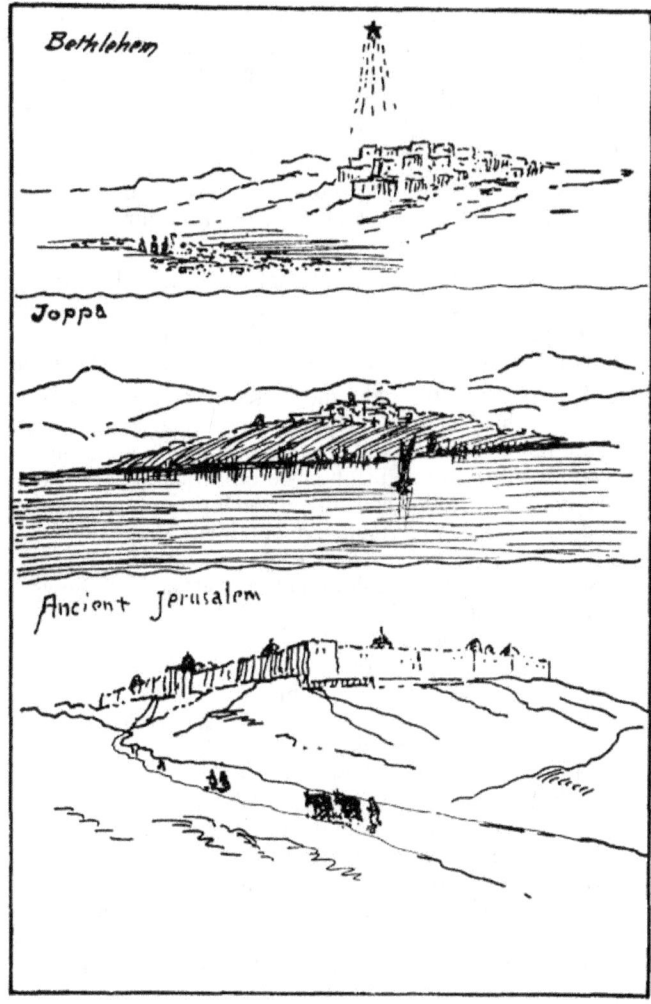

A night effect on the upper picture is secured either by having a gray paper or by first coating your paper with gray chalk, then making outlines in black. Use light yellow for star, rays of light, and reflections on houses and lights from windows. The simple lines give perspective.

The bright colors of springtime and summer—the deep-blue sky, the brilliant green grass and foliage, and the blossoms and flowers—present an entirely different color harmony from that of the haze of autumn days, when the frosts have turned the leaves to amber and gold, and the foliage and grass have taken on a more somber shade.

But the bright autumn colors compare with the brilliant sunset, in that they are short-lived and changes rapidly take place.

The winter landscape presents an altogether different value in color schemes. Even the deep greens of the evergreen harmonize with the drab tree trunks and seemingly dead foliage and branches, and the snow adds a finish to the picture.

This *is* an age of color, and more brilliant tints and shades are used than formerly. This is exemplified in almost every phase of business and life. It is therefore quite in keeping with modern times to use brighter colors in chalk work; but by the proper application and correct combinations of colors better and more pleasing effects are obtained.

Some very pleasing color combinations are as follows:
Brown, orange, black.
Orange, gray, black.
Gray, red, black, yellow.
Green, purple, blue, yellow, black.
Orange, blue, dull green, brown, white.
Bright yellow, deep blue, dark gray blue, black.
Tan, purple, blue, dark brown, black.
Light blue, deep blue, white, black, orange, tan.
Dull lemon yellow, orange, blue, deep blue, black.
Deep green, bright green, brown, lavender, cream.
Dark blue, deep blue, white, black, orange, tan.
Lavender, deep green, light green, bright yellow, white, black.

There is no fixed rule to govern the coloring of your

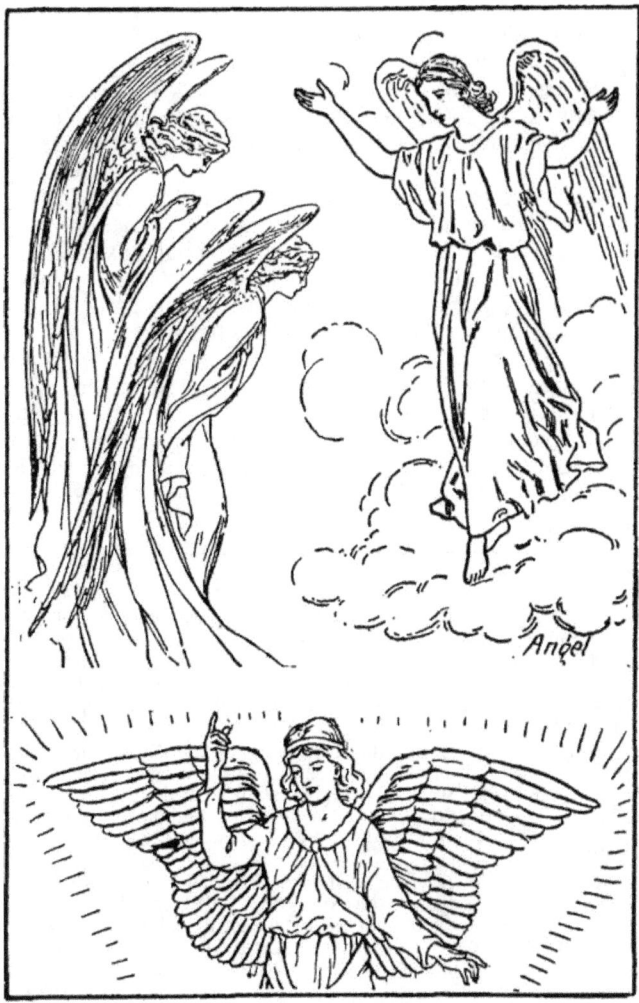

Here are several good sketches for practice. All these are good subjects and should be drawn several times. It is a good idea to draw these sketches with pencil first and then with crayon.

drawings. You may use a combination of colors which will help to emphasize your sketch.

When lettering is used with a drawing, it is well to use certain colors for certain words. See chapter on "Colors and Their Meaning," in this book. A few suggestions are here given.

Trust and love: Pink, blended down to lighter shade.

Truth: Blue, blended down to lighter shade.

Joy: Gold or orange, blended down to lighter shade.

Purity: Should be white. This may be obtained by making letters in outline and using some color on the ground outside and surrounding the strokes of the letters.

Danger: Red.

Hatred, betrayal, sin, wickedness: Yellow, green, brown, red, and black.

If time will permit, an elaborate drawing may be produced with ordinary assorted colored school crayons or chalk. These crayons may be purchased at any stationer's or school supply store.

SEE PAGE 65

Carefully draw the first picture and compare the figures with trouble and trials of life. If we look at failure that is all we can see. Everything looks dark and gloomy, but remember every shadow has a light behind it; so when we feel discouraged we should look up toward the light. Then complete the face on the side toward the light, block out the first face, and finish the picture.

A good stunt against the use of cigarettes. Begin with C, then follow with the I and G, being careful to place them in their proper, respective places so as to make the skull face; then follow with the rest of the word and end with the cigarette, and make the smoke by encircling the contour of the top of the head and ending at the base of the fag.

Expressions of the face are but the manipulations of marks. Note how simple lines change the expression. This is the simplest form of facial expression. It looks easy, and it is easy to make. Take your pencil and a piece of paper and try it. First make the circle, then the eyes, nose, and mouth; then the marks on the cheeks—see how this changes the expression.

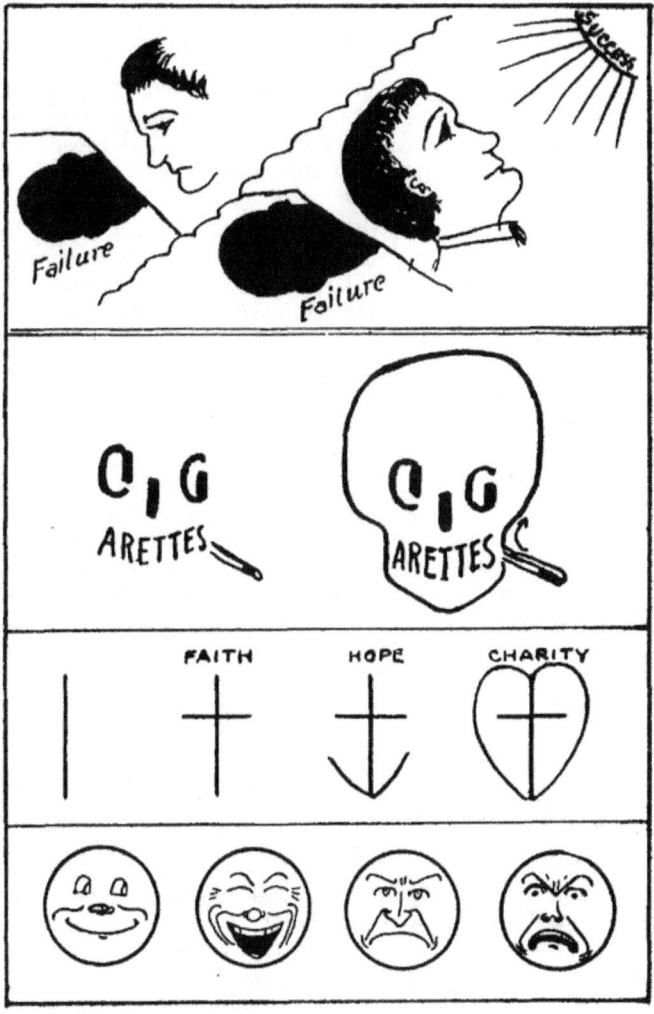

See explanation at bottom of page 64,

COLORS AND THEIR MEANING

Colored crayons may be used to a decided advantage in chalk-talk work, since each of the different colors has a definite meaning, established by constant use throughout the centuries. It is well that we understand something about color and its meaning before attempting to make color drawings.

There are a number of passages in the Bible referring to color; also, the pages of history contain many references to colors and their meaning. The old masters demonstrated their knowledge of color in their work which we prize today as art treasures.

Day and night have played quite an important part in many of the religions of the past. They are represented by black and white and are identified with good and evil.

White has always represented purity, and in many countries of today white signifies divine perfection. The Jewish high priests in Moses' time wore white robes. In many of the religious festivities in which girls or virgins play an important part, white is always worn. Christ's raiment at the time of his transfiguration is described as "white as the light"; also, when he appeared to John on the Isle of Patmos, even his face and hair were "white like wool." John also described the great multitudes in heaven as being clothed in white, and the bride of Christ, representing the church, was dressed in white.

Artists of medieval times always painted God in white, as well as the Virgin Mary at the annunciation and Jesus at the resurrection. These same artists sometimes portrayed Christ as wearing a black robe during the period of his temptation. Joel says, "All faces shall gather blackness"—meaning terror, or fright. The third horse which John saw in his vision was black, and it is said to represent famine.

In some of the foreign countries, brown is the color of mourning. It is the color of the barren earth, of dead trees,

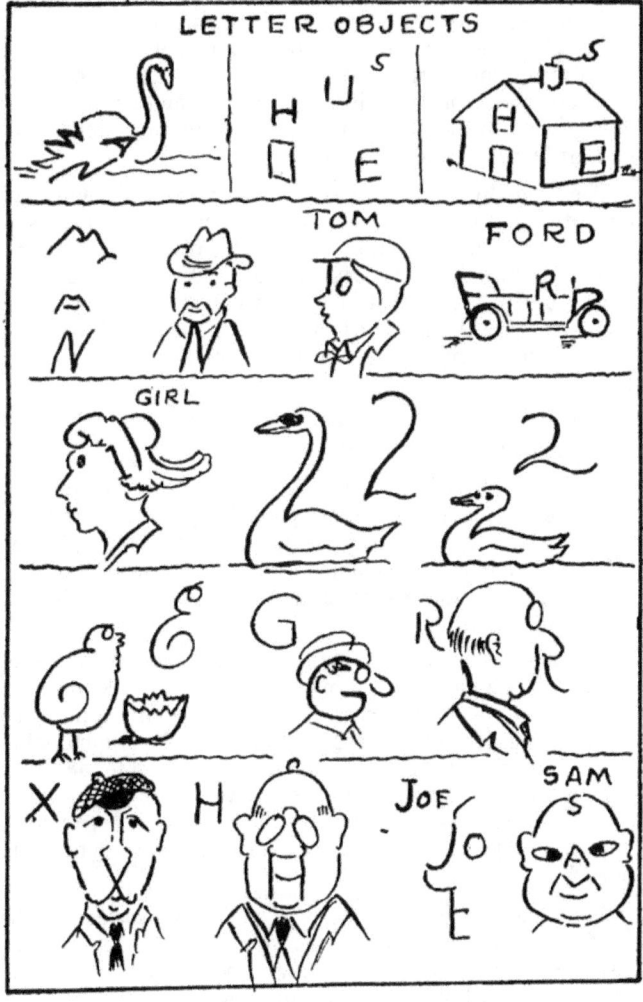

In each of the above the letter or the figure is made first, being carefully placed in the correct position, and then the rest of the picture is drawn. This is good practice and always interesting.

and withered leaves; and since it is a mixture of orange, white, and black, it has been closely associated with black as a symbol of suffering and sorrow. It was the one color worn by the Quakers as a protest against worldliness and show. Brown and gray form the principal garb worn in monasteries as a sign of humility and penitence.

The blue sky has always stood for truth. In the Old Testament a number of references are made to the word "sapphire" (blue) in connection with God himself, and blue has always been associated with trueness. We say a person is "true blue." It is said that the flower called the forget-me-not was thus named because of its color, as a symbol of constancy. Painters in olden times gave Christ and the Virgin Mary blue garments.

Blue is also called a cold color. For instance, people with a gloomy disposition have the "blues."

As the earth is clothed in its splendid garb of green leaves and grass, green has been accepted as symbolizing fertility, fruitfulness, and prosperity. David declares of the righteous: "He shall be like a tree planted by the rivers of water ... his leaf also shall not wither; and whatsoever he doeth shall prosper."

The martyrs were often painted with green palms in their hands, representing victory over death. Spring celebrates her victory over winter by appearing in a garment of green foliage, representing life. Evergreens are the symbol of immortality. Green has also another meaning, being used to designate dishonesty and signify any destructive or malicious force. Shakespeare, in the *Merchant of Venice,* speaks of "green-eyed jealousy"; and a common expression is "green with envy."

In Oriental countries yellow was closely associated with the sun and its worshipers. It was the royal color of China. Gold is also the symbol of the sun. Yellow is the nearest color to gold; therefore they both have the same meaning.

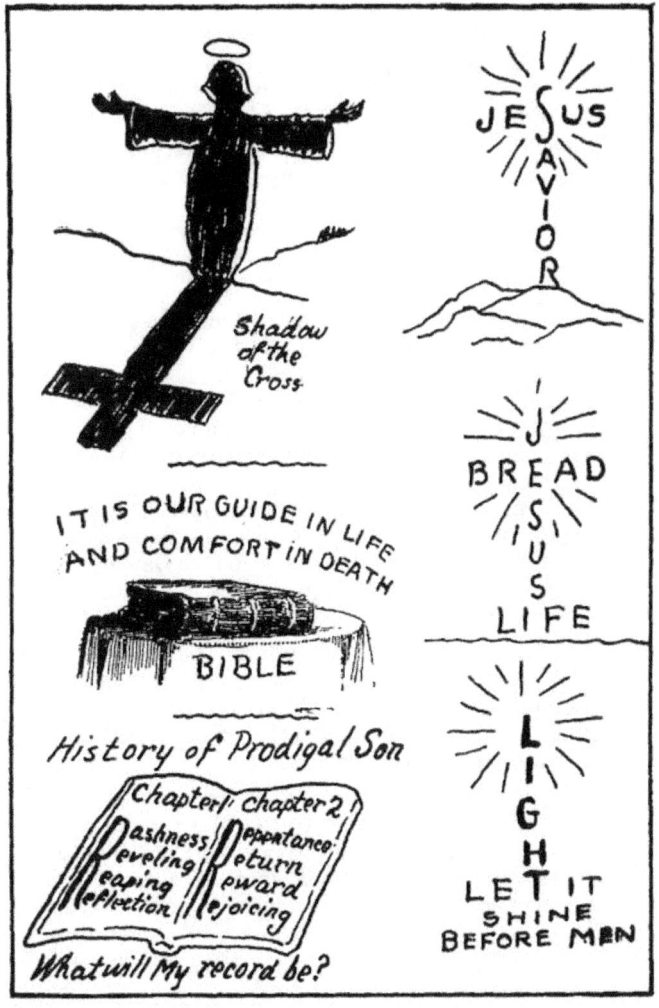

Shadow of the Cross

IT IS OUR GUIDE IN LIFE AND COMFORT IN DEATH

BIBLE

History of Prodigal Son

Chapter 1
Rashness
Reveling
Reaping
Reflection

Chapter 2
Repentance
Return
Reward
Rejoicing

What will My record be?

JESUS SAVIOR

JESUS BREAD LIFE

LIGHT LET IT SHINE BEFORE MEN

First make the sketch of the body of Christ standing in the sunlight; then the shadow—the cross. Build a story around each of the other sketches.

The streets of the New Jerusalem are pure gold, according to John's description as they appeared to him while he "was in the Spirit" on the Isle of Patmos. He also said, "The city was pure gold, like unto glass"; that is to say, like yellow light.

The yellow fields of corn and grain represent the wisdom of God. The paintings of the old masters gave Jacob a yellow robe because of his wisdom in obeying the angels. The opposite meaning is often used when describing a dishonest person: "He is yellow." Artists have often pictured Judas Iscariot as wearing robes of dirty yellow.

Inasmuch as orange is the color that most nearly represents fire, it was extensively used by the fire worshipers. It signifies wisdom. The lighted lamp held in the hand is a symbol of human knowledge. Fire on the hearth is referred to as a symbol of hospitality, and the orange-colored flame is the symbol of the Spirit. God manifested himself to Moses in the burning bush. He went before the Israelites in a pillar of fire by night. He descended on Mount Sinai in fire, and his divine presence was likewise made manifest in the Tabernacle in the wilderness. The Spirit's coming on the Day of Pentecost was also represented as "cloven tongues like as of fire" that "sat upon each of them."

Yet fire, symbolized by the orange color, though it is a good servant, is a bad master and very destructive in its uncontrolled state. Orange and black are the colors generally attributed to Satan, and orange and black are colors common to various venomous reptiles and insects.

Life in the blood, whose symbol is red, signifies love. Red has stood for love in all the countries of the earth. The robes worn by high priests at times were red, and the color of a cardinal's robe is bright red. Red is more often symbolically used in literature than any other color. In the Old Testament red is referred to as representing love, and some of the old masters in art painted a red robe on Mary Magdalene. The

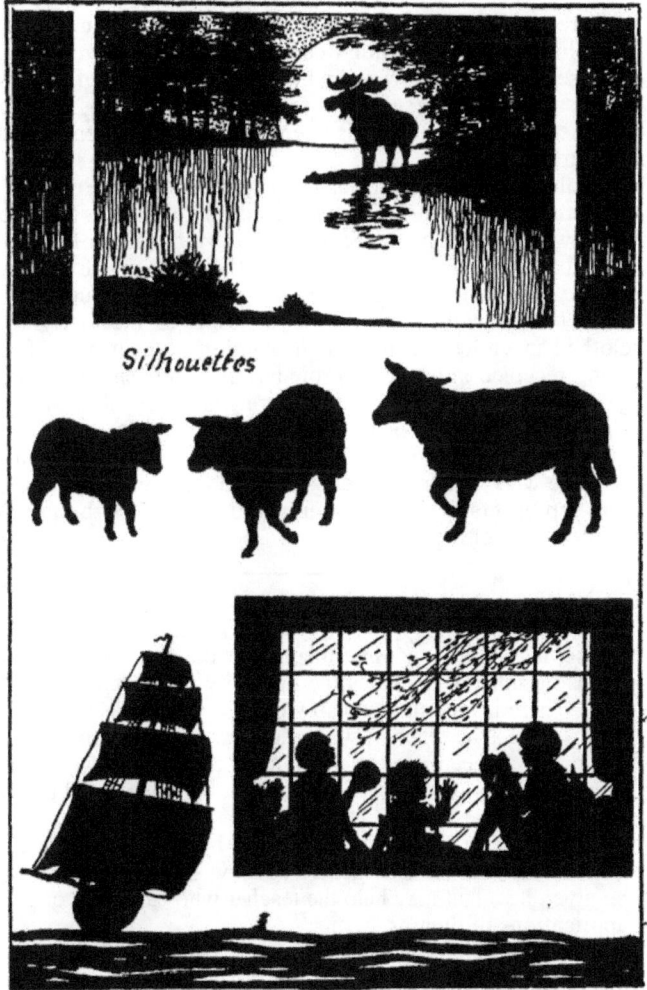

Silhouettes

These pictures are called silhouettes. They give the effect of looking at objects which are between you and the light. This kind of drawing is always effective.

pictures of the Madonna, almost without exception, are red and blue, for love and truth. Red also has an opposite meaning, representing war and crime. In his vision on the Isle of Patmos, John saw the red horse of war followed by the black horse of famine. The red dragon, also seen by John, represented evil, war, and crime.

Violet and purple are often used synonymously. Purple is a mixture of red and blue. Violet is a bluish purple, and is the color of flowers by that name. Since violet is a mixture of red and blue, or love and truth, it represents the color of the Son and the Father. Old masters gave Jesus a violet robe, to suggest his perfect union with God; they also portrayed the martyrs as clothed in violet during their martyrdom, but in white after being received in heaven. Purple has always been the color of garments and robes worn by sovereigns on royal occasions. Violet is also the symbol of sorrow, sadness, and mourning. Not the mourning of those who have no hope, but the mourning of those who "endure as seeing Him who is invisible." Violet also represents the day as it draws to an end, as the purple shades of evening.

CRAYON IN THE SUNDAY SCHOOL

Keeping junior and intermediate children busy and their minds occupied often taxes the ingenuity of the teacher to the limit. There is nothing that can yield such results as the crayon in this case. The teacher, when he finds that something must be done to concentrate the thoughts of the boys and girls, can resort to the use of the chalk, a supply of which should always be kept ready at hand.

A number of little "stunts" should be practiced over and over beforehand for emergencies. A few suggestive ideas will be given here that may help the teacher who can make original applications of them.

With your chalk first make a large capital J at the upper left corner of your paper, and ask what boy it was who had

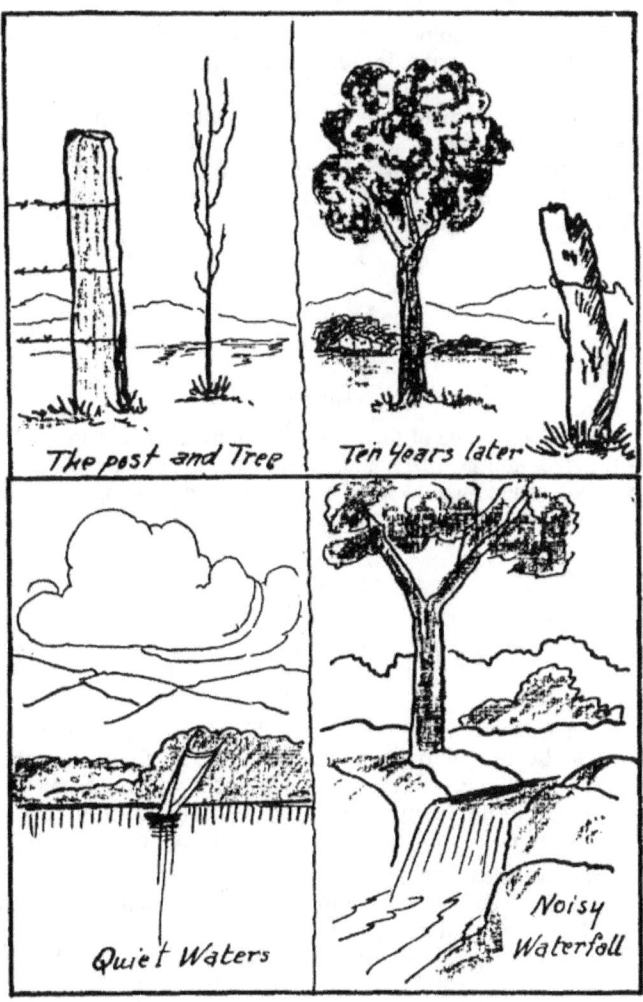

A few simple illustrations easy to make, but impressive if used rightly. Explained in the text. See page 80.

a coat of many colors, or what boy was sold into Egypt. As soon as Joseph's name is mentioned, make the other letters of the name in a line below the first one on the sheet. Now ask the class to name some good trait of character Joseph had that begins with the letter J. The word "just" could be used. Ask what other trait he had which begins with O. "Obedient" can be used for the second letter. Then sincere, earnest, patient, and honest, thus.

> J   ust
> O   bedient
> S   incere
> E   arnest
> P   atient
> . H   onest

Then turn to one of the class, preferably the one who is least attentive, and ask, "Thomas, how would you like to *live* so that your name would stand for some splendid things ? Let us see what the name Thomas might stand for."

> T   ruthful
> H   onest
> O   rderly
> M   anly
> A   mbitious S
> teady

The teacher can comment on what a splendid record that would be for anyone and remark that he feels sure that Thomas will measure up to every bit of it. Thus a lesson will be taught to the pupils. An apt teacher will adapt an unlimited number of such ideas to fit the occasion.

Another idea may be adapted to suit almost any Bible story or incident. Draw a picture of a boat to represent the ark and ask the class what person or incident in the Bible it suggests. The answer *is,* "Noah." A basket in some bushes: "Moses." Pole with serpent: "Israelites in the wilderness."

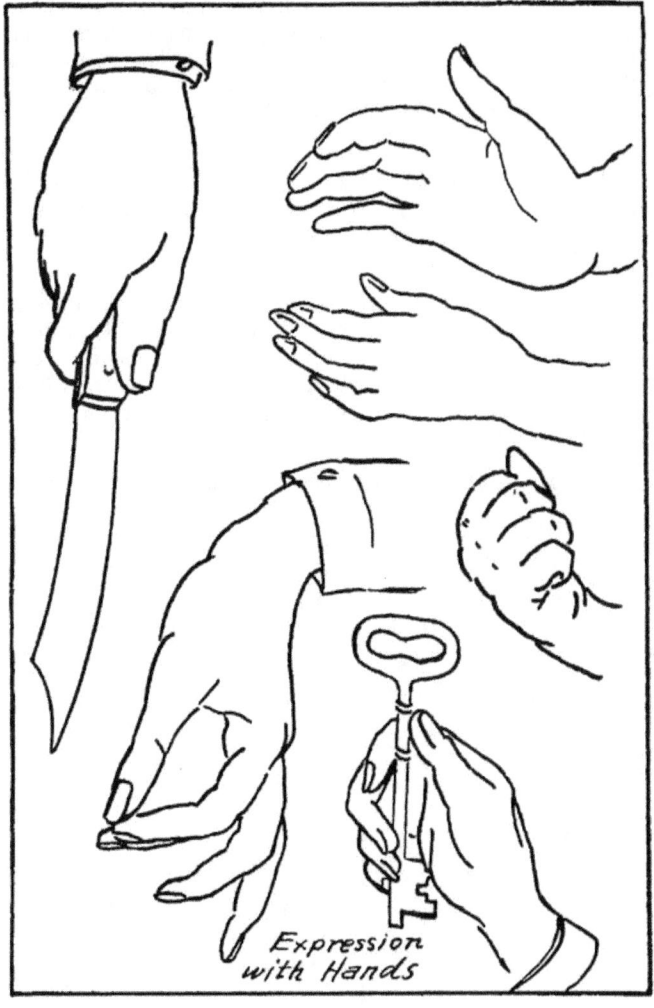

Expression with Hands

Ladies' hands and men's hands, in almost every shape. Try making them just as near like the original as possible.

Some lamps: "Parable of the Ten Virgins." Broom: "The Parable of the Lost Coin." An apple: "The Garden of Eden." Dove: "The Flood." Raven: "Elijah." Tables of stone: "Moses." Sling: "David." Star: "Bethlehem Babe." Cross: "The Crucifixion."

To conduct this with interest let the class choose sides; then ask each side a question. If answered correctly, it gives the side one point to their credit. If one side fails to answer a question, let the other side try it.

There are many ways in which crayon pictures or words may be varied for people of different ages, and for different occasions. For instance, a sketch of a fish net may be used in finding out how many of the pupils know which of Christ's disciples were fishermen; or a tent will bring up the subject of Paul and his trade.

Names of Bible characters may be made into an acrostic, as

> D aniel
> A mos
> N ahum
> I saiah
> E zakiel
> L aban

Who were they? Tell about them.

Here is another acrostic:

> C heerful
> H onest
> R epentant
> I ndustrious
> S ubmissive
> T ruthful
> I nnocent
> A ffectionate
> N oble

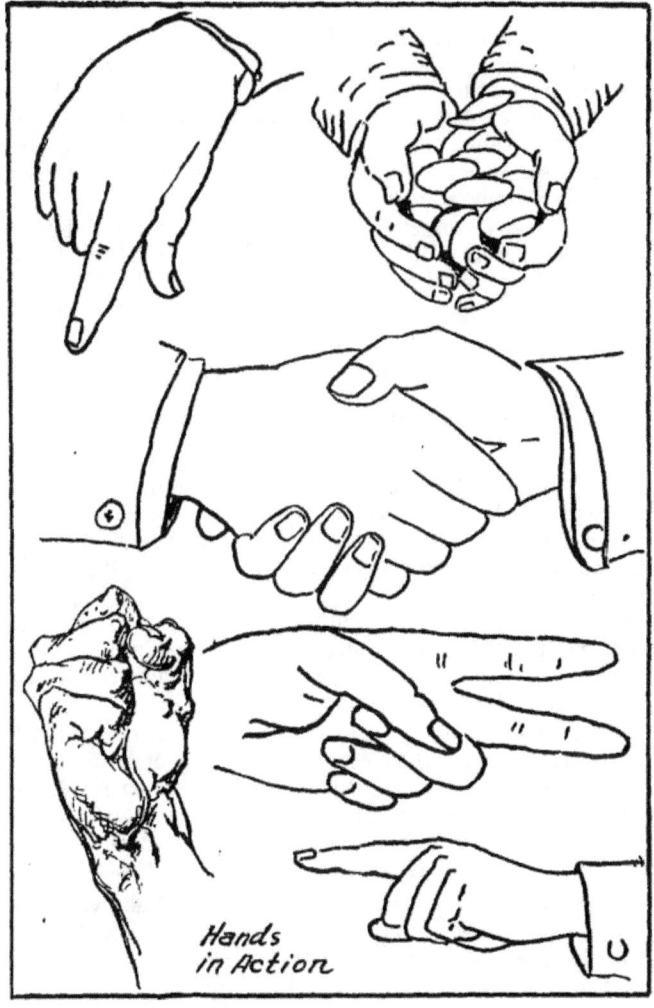

Hands
in Action

Note the shaded effect of the fist. The same shading may be added to any of the rest with good effect. A simple statement in crude lettering is strengthened 100 per cent by the addition of a well-worked-out hand in one of the shapes here shown.

To illustrate a good point about keeping a secret when but one knows it, we indicate it thus: (1). But if we tell it to another person, that makes two ones (11), or eleven. From this may be explained why so many secrets leak out when told. But this same rule holds good when we tell the gospel truths to someone (1) ; the good news is so good that it soon spreads to someone else (11).

Also, God is something, as (1). We are as nothing (0) when compared to him; but if we place God first in our lives, if we get on the right side of God (10), he magnifies us and we multiply him. If we place ourselves first, let us see what the result will be (01).

When our will and God's will run parallel (=), there is equality and harmony; but when our will runs contrary to God's will, then come the crosses (+) of life.

There are several good object lessons that may be learned by considering light. The Bible says, "Ye are the light of the world." We are as the candle, lamp, or electric globe. Not one of these can ignite itself—we cannot light ourselves spiritually. When the candle is lit, or as soon as the electric current begins to flow through the light bulb, it begins to shine. Immediately upon being lighted we shine for Christ, for he is the power within that causes us to shine. The Bible does not say we are to "make our light shine"; but we are simply to "let it shine."

The candle or electric globe shines for others; we are to shine that others may be blessed. The lamp is constantly giving up its own life in service to others; so we must sacrifice self to serve others. One lamp in working order can give light to hundreds and lose none of its brightness—it shines just as brightly in cellar, parlor, pulpit, or out of doors.

The moon is also spoken of as a source of light, yet it too, like the cold incandescent lamp, has no light within itself. It merely takes the light that it receives from the great source and speeds it on its way, to be a blessing to others.

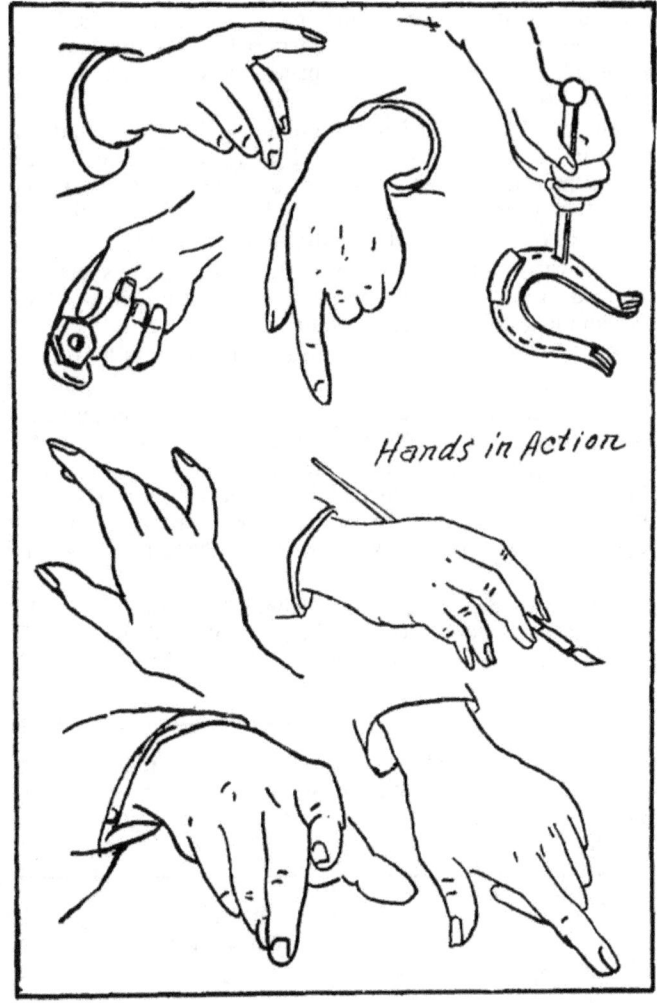

Hands in Action

No part of the human form is used in illustration more than the hand, and on these four pages of hand illustrations you will find hands in almost any position. Practice all of them, for they will be valuable.

A picture of a tree and a post may be made side by side. At first the tree is small and slender; but it has life and will eventually grow to be useful to man. It gets larger and sturdier and of more service. (See page 73.)

The post, when put into the ground, is large and solid and supports a fence. But it is dead, and the forces of nature begin their destructive work upon it—it begins to decay, and in a few years rots off and falls to earth. The difference between the two is: one is alive, and the other is dead.

The varied characteristics of life and its laws may be likened to the forces of good and evil exemplified by those which make for good or ill in the tree and post.

See sketch on page 73; then go on with this lesson.

First draw the quiet, slow-moving, deep river, with the sailboat, and tell of the silent but powerful waters that flow on through the ages to bless generations of men. Then tell about going into the woods and hearing falling waters. Compare the noisy little stream with the mighty, silent river, and compare people with small minds who cause trouble and agitation in a community with people who are noble, charitable, kind, and sensible.

Here is another little stunt called the "Golden Rule." Ask a pupil to assist you. Give him the piece of chalk and ask him to draw as straight a line as he can, from left to right across the board.

Now ask, "Is that straight?" It will more than likely be crooked in places. Now tell him that you will fasten a string across the board with a tack at each end, as a guide for his hand.

Now ask him to draw a perfectly straight line, using the string as a guide for his hand. Of course, the string gives, and the line is as crooked as ever.

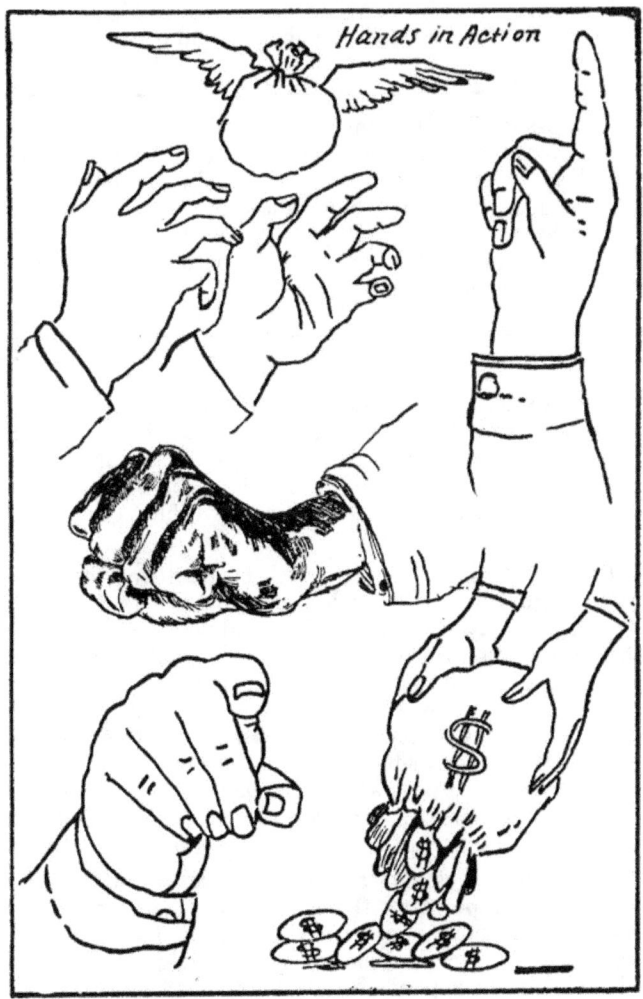

Action is expressed by the hand to as great an extent as by any other part of the body. Here is the shaded fist. Note the high light and shadow. Try this shading on one of the other hands.

Now take a yardstick, or straightedge, and draw a perfectly straight line.

The lesson: We all want to live perfectly straight lives; we do not want to make crooked work of it. If we depend on ourselves, we are likely to have crooked lives. Following the string is like trying to follow someone else who *is* as weak and faulty as ourselves. There is a rule that will keep us straight—we call it the Golden Rule, because it is so good and it is as valuable as gold.

Now ask the pupil to draw lines on both sides of the rule. These are parallel lines; we should draw the lines for others as we would draw them for ourselves—parallel lines. (See Matthew 7:12.) Build a very profitable lesson around this by getting the class to find the verse in their Bibles. Get them to commit the verse to memory.

In years of Sunday-school work I have found that some lessons yield to an illustration well, but others do not. In standing before an audience of old and young, I have found that as soon as I picked up the piece of chalk interest was aroused; and as the different marks and lines were made, every pair of eyes followed each move. Regardless of what was said, the lesson brought out by the chalk was what impressed the minds of the audience. I know this to be true, for time and again boys and girls have reminded me of some diagram or picture I had made years before. I have found, therefore, that the result of the chalk is successful and lasting.

In work among children and young people, in school, Sunday school, young people's meetings, clubs, entertainments, and homes, the opportunities of impressing good seed thoughts with chalk were never better. A great many illustrations and pictures may be applied and adapted to good advantage.

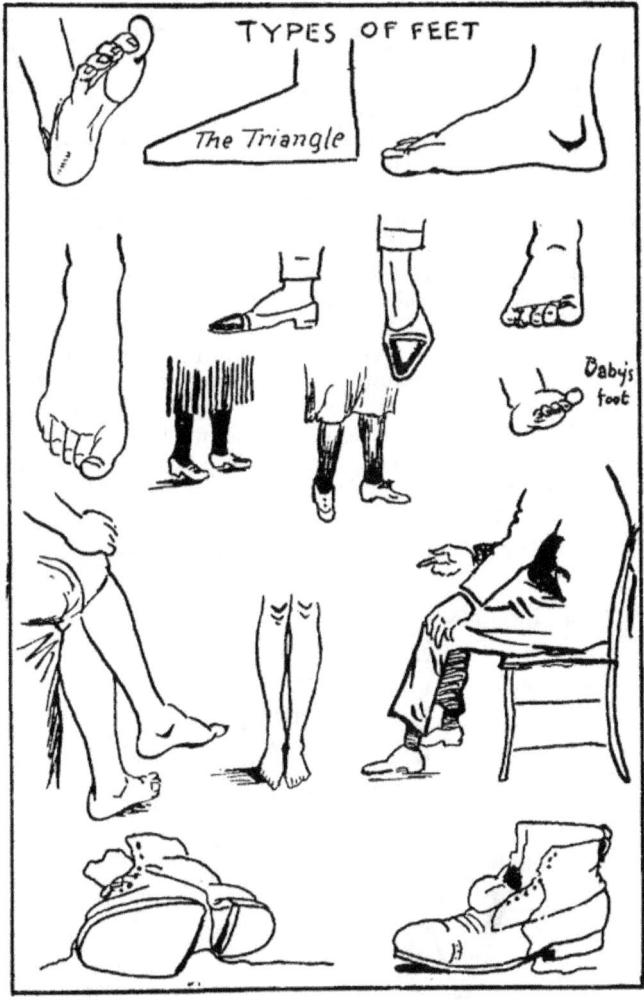

The bare foot is rarely drawn in public pictures, but it is important. If the foot or shoe is improperly drawn, it gives an awkward appearance to the whole picture.

It is not necessary to produce a work of art in order to be appreciated, for even the cartoonists and comic strip artists of today use illustrations that appeal to the common people and are full of human interest.

The common things of life, which have always interested the masses, are what made the teachings of Jesus of Nazareth so gripping. He gave word pictures of the commonplace things about him and drew from them lessons that the people of his day could understand. He talked of the lilies, ravens, sparrows, chickens, vineyards, cornfields, and fishermen; of money, children, and many other things about which the people had definite knowledge. He talked to the common people on their own level and in their own realm of understanding. Even the children could understand his teachings, as well as the older people. The children can understand them now. All these lessons may be impressed on the minds of children by the use of a piece of chalk. The chalk can be made to impress indelibly each incident of a lesson in a way that will help build character and a foundation for a useful life.

Here are a few more acrostics that are interesting:

***

Word of God—

B OOK OF BOOKS
I NSPIRED OF GOD
B LESSED TRUTH
L AMP OF LIFE
E TERNAL WORD

***

Good motto—

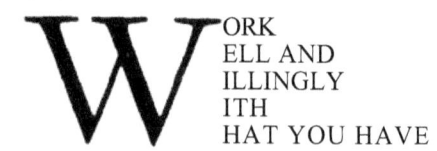

W ORK
ELL AND
ILLINGLY
ITH
HAT YOU HAVE

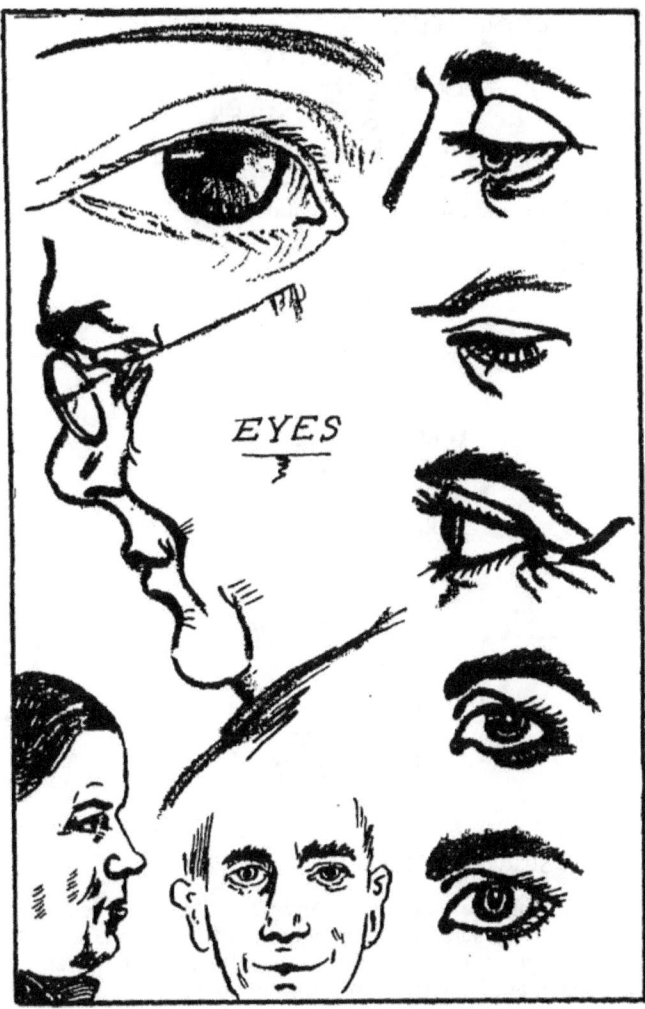

EYES

The eye is the index to the face, and of all things must be carefully drawn. Still there is nothing difficult about drawing it. You should put much practice on eyes.

Though we should suffer

INJUSTICE
HATRED
SICKNESS
TROUBLES
SORROWS

Let JESUS shine forth in the midst of trials.

* * *

Matt. 7:7—

ASK
SEEK
KNOCK

* * *

P ERSISTENTLY
R EGULARLY
A RDENTLY
Y EARNINGLY

* * *

BE {
H ONORABLE
U SEFUL
M EEK
B ENEFICENT
L OVING
E ARNEST
}

A SCRAPBOOK OF ILLUSTRATIONS

One of the handiest things for any person who wishes to do chalk work is a scrap box, scrapbook, or file of some sort.

For many years I have had such a collection, to which many sketches and designs are added from time to time. Many

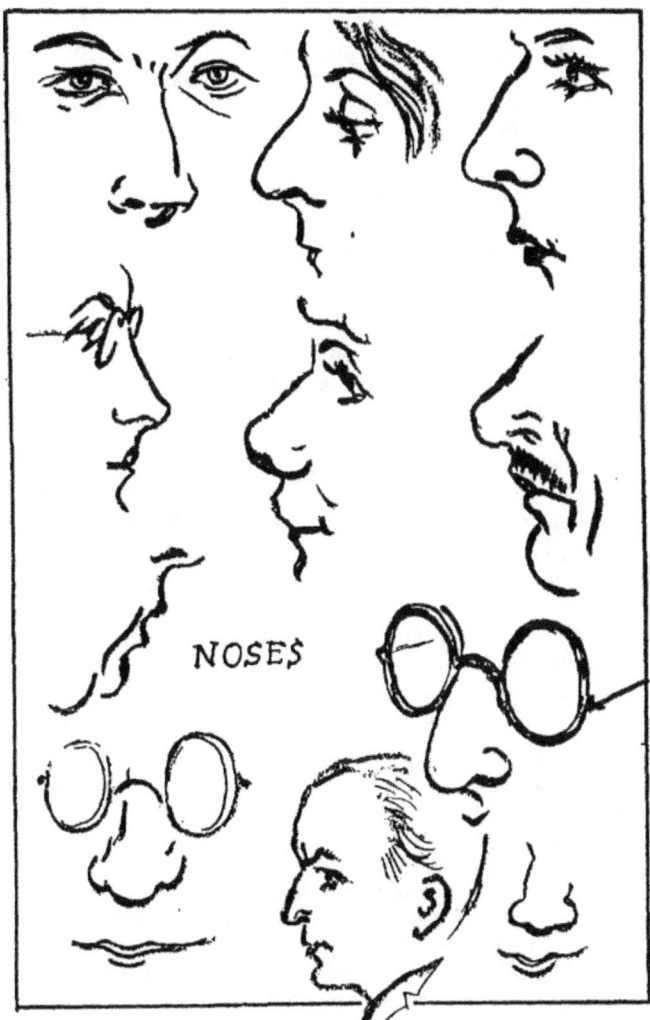

The curves of the nose as well as the eye, ear, and mouth must be carefully drawn. Try drawing some types of noses you see every day, which are not shown here.

of the sketches in this book are drawn from this collection. It is well to have envelopes of uniform size, either the kind for catalogs or legal use (known as No. 10). A box large enough to permit these envelopes to stand on edge is the handiest.

The envelopes are used to classify the different kinds of clippings, such as flowers, birds, buildings, landscapes, and people. Whenever an illustration from a magazine or newspaper can be clipped, so much the better; but where this is impossible, an outline on thin paper may be made of such portions of it as promise to be useful. If a sheet of carbon paper is available, lay it under the illustration and on a sheet of paper to take the transfer, and by a pointed instrument or pencil trace the outlines. Where carbon paper is not available, cover a space on a sheet of paper with lead pencil markings, using a flat portion of lead; this will serve as carbon and will transfer quite plainly. A pantagraph is a handy instrument for copying sketches in any proportionate size.

With such a collection of material, any person will soon have a wealth of illustrative matter from which chalk pictures may be adapted. It is well also to make pencil sketches of chalk talks used in your own public work and mark on these the date and where used. This is valuable for reference.

Occasionally the representation of an eye, or hand, or some other detail of the human figure seems almost a necessity in blackboard teaching and sketching. Such details are difficult unless you have a good collection of eyes, hands, feet, and such like from which you can select a sketch that is suitable. It would be well to practice on these, as a hand or eye without the proper shape and effect appears awkward. Almost everyone knows how they should look to be natural, and if they are made incorrectly they will be very noticeable; however, after a little practice in producing a good sketch the job is easy. The sketches of the hand and other parts of the human figure given in this book are very valuable.

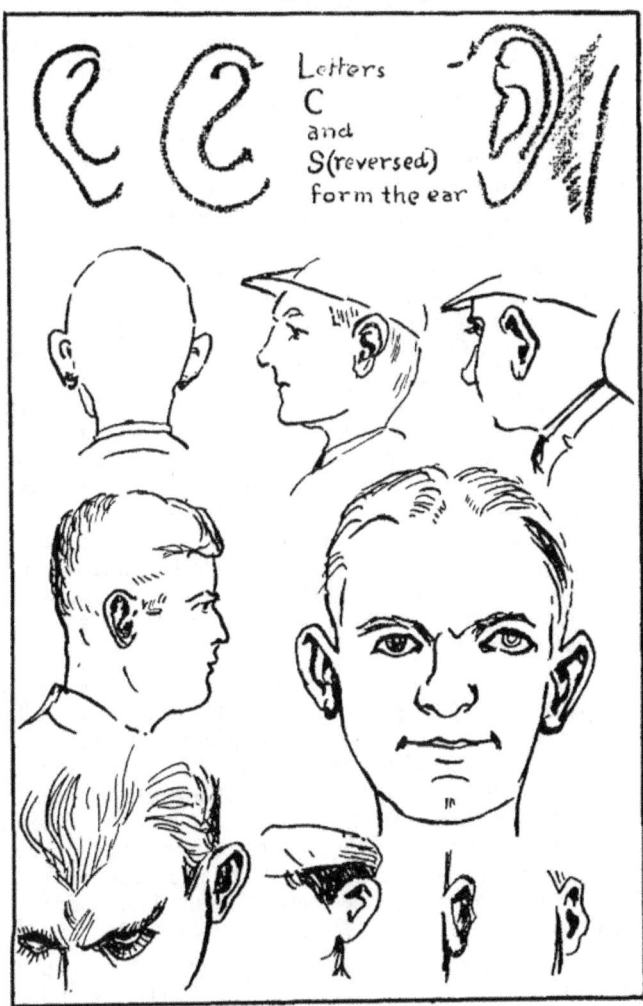

The ear is like the C and S (reversed) and must be drawn carefully. There are many shapes of ears, and much practice should be given the ear.

There are some lessons that will not yield to illustration very well, but with a little thought some suitable sketch, diagram, acrostic, or outline will suggest itself to your mind.

Take, for instance, the story of Christmas—a sketch similar to the one given in this book may be made before the class in such a way that it will impress some truths on the minds of the youth in a manner that will never be forgotten. Here is a sketch of Bethlehem. (See page 61.) In order to make a night scene you should cover with a bluish gray the entire portion of the sheet of paper which your picture will occupy. Rub the chalk on chamois or cotton and apply the color to the paper with a circular motion in such a way that the entire surface will be covered with gray. Then with a black crayon draw the hill country and the old-fashioned village with flat-roofed houses of stone—all the while telling of the Eastern custom of caring for flocks of sheep in the open country and on the hillsides, and how the shepherds were watching over their flocks by night when the angel of the Lord appeared and brought the glad tidings to the shepherds. Locate a particular spot where the Christ child lay and above it make the star and also the rays of light in yellow, and some spots of dim light coming from the windows. Make these also in yellow or light orange.

Such a picture has great possibilities. It impresses on the minds of the audience the nature of that hilly country. The ancient dwellings and the star of Bethlehem are made more vivid than they could possibly be by a fully colored printed picture. The mere fact that the audience has seen it produced, together with the story, makes it doubly interesting and deeply impresses the thought on their minds. A photograph or finely printed picture cannot yield so much; it cannot follow the unfolding truth, as does the chalk, from the first mark representing the hills, then houses, and finally the star.

The simple story, from the prophecy of the star to the light that shines in our hearts, is full of interest, and any

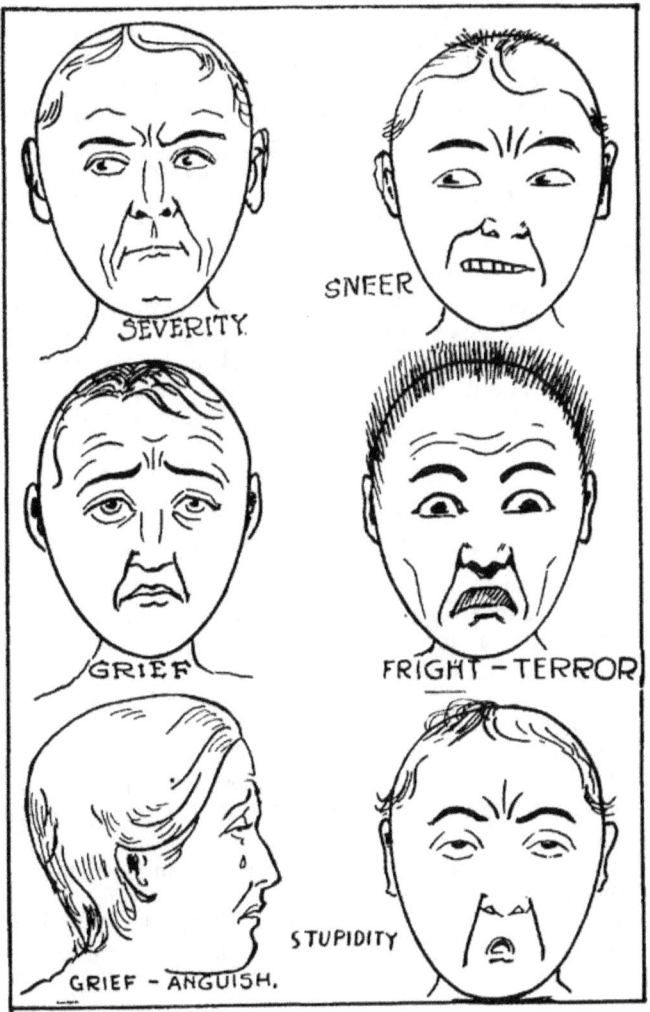

These are called egg-shaped faces, and the contour is practically the same in the various faces. This is good practice work, and you will always find good use for knowledge of how to produce the multitude of facial expressions.

teacher should easily see how the chalk can help in teaching the simple truths. The high lights, or reflection of the moon on the roofs of the buildings, can be made to add interest to the scene by touching up with yellow, only it should be used sparingly.

The Bethlehem scene is only one of hundreds of such lessons in the Bible that yield to illustration. There is scarcely a Sunday-school lesson, or any subject one desires to dwell upon, but that may be adapted to some scene, diagram, or outline.

Suggestions and outlines of subjects would fill many books; in fact there are several books of this kind on the market, if one desires such material, but to have a knowledge such as this book imparts is worth far more to you than outlines, since you learn to adapt your own ideas and designs to your drawing.

WHAT IS MEANT BY PERSPECTIVE

The meaning of the word "perspective" is given as the "art or science of representing, on a surface, objects as they actually appear to the eye."

Sometimes a very few lines or marks, or the position and size of certain objects, will give the effect of distance, without which the picture would appear flat.

In order to become a successful chalk talker, blackboard illustrator, or even an occasional user of the chalk, we must of necessity know a few of the technical terms and understand them.

As you stand on the beach looking far out to sea over the blue waters, your eyes come to a point where the sky and water meet—we call this line the horizon. The effect is the same when looking out over a plain, desert, or prairie.

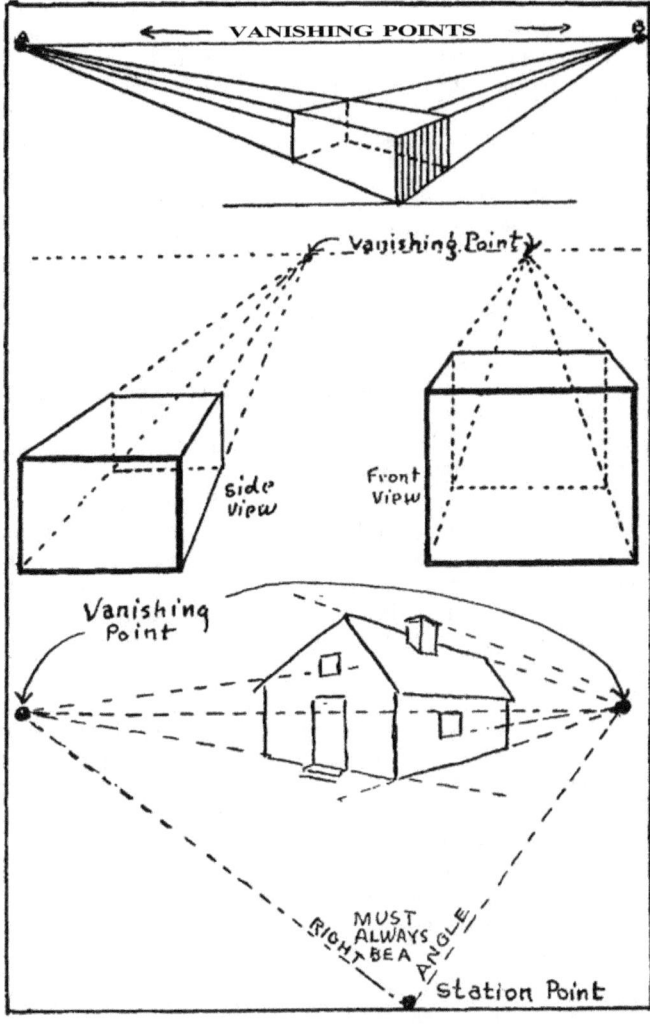

Here is the simplest demonstration of perspective known. Read explanation in the text and study it out for yourself. This will not be difficult, because it is as plain as the nose on a face after you see these pictures.

The horizon line must appear in every out-of-door picture, or any picture where the artist wishes to indicate distance. The true horizon usually appears at the level of the eye from where the person is standing. There is no set rule as to just where this line shall appear in the picture; it is usually either a little above or a little below the center. Look carefully over the sketches in this chapter.

All parallel lines that recede from us converge at a point somewhere on the horizon, and this is known as the vanishing point, or point of sight. For instance, standing on a railroad track and looking as far as the eyes can see, the two rails approach each other. The effect is noted when standing in the middle of a long street. Trees or telephone poles, when standing in a long row, seem gradually to diminish in size as they go farther away from us. (See the illustrations on this point.) The point of sight is usually about five feet above the ground, and every level line points toward a spot level with your eye.

Considering all that has been said about perspective, the student may at first have become somewhat bewildered, and the whole subject may seem complicated. This is the way one writer explains perspective: "All level lines leading away from the observer vanish at a point on the horizon which is level with the eye of the observer." This is an almost infallible rule; if memorized and put to practice it will banish all doubts and fears.

You will notice that lines on the building (page 93) lead to the vanishing point, and even the doors, windows, and chimney point to the same spot. If you were standing in a street looking down the rows of tall buildings, and you wanted to make a sketch of the scene, all lines, such as rows of windows, doors, and cornice would extend to this same point.

There are a number of variations between what is called the natural vanishing point and the accidental vanishing point,

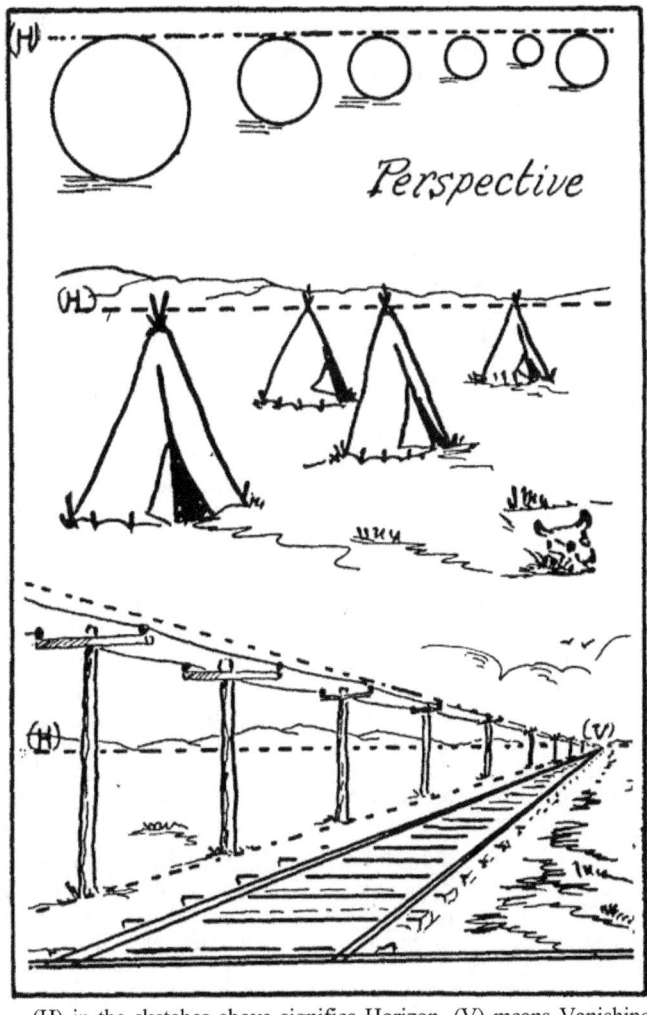

Perspective

(H) in the sketches above signifies Horizon. (V) means Vanishing Point referred to in this chapter. In Sketch No. 1 the balls touch the horizon line, as do the tepees in No. 2. This arrangement alone gives perspective to the sketches.

but these cannot be explained here. The simplest perspective illustration is the drawing of the boxes in this chapter. Study this sketch thoroughly, and you will find the rules of perspective really easy.

Perspective in landscape is largely brought about by comparative objects and the size in which they are indicated. Often a sailboat in the distance, even though it be but a mere mark, puts the finishing touch to the picture, and it appears that you are looking miles away into the distance.

There are two distance points—one at the right side, and the other at the left of the vanishing point, or point of sight. All lines which do not converge at the point of sight do so at the distance points, or at the vanishing points fixed by the position of the object.

The place where we stand is called the station point, and is not within the picture, but at such a point where the picture can be viewed to good advantage. It is similar to the distance points, in that they are entirely out of the picture, yet control the perspective.

The lower edge of the picture, or more positive position, or surface on which the objects stand, is called the ground line. It is represented by a straight line parallel with the horizon.

There are also other terms, such as the perspective plane, which is the distance between the horizon and ground line; the central visual ray, which is the line from the station point to the point of sight, and other technical terms, a knowledge of which is absolutely necessary in the study of professional art. Any person wishing to learn more of this interesting subject will find instructive material in the libraries.

It is the object of this book to give only the limited amount of such information necessary to enable the chalk talker to make drawings above the novice class. By carefully examining the illustrations in this chapter this whole subject will be easily understood.

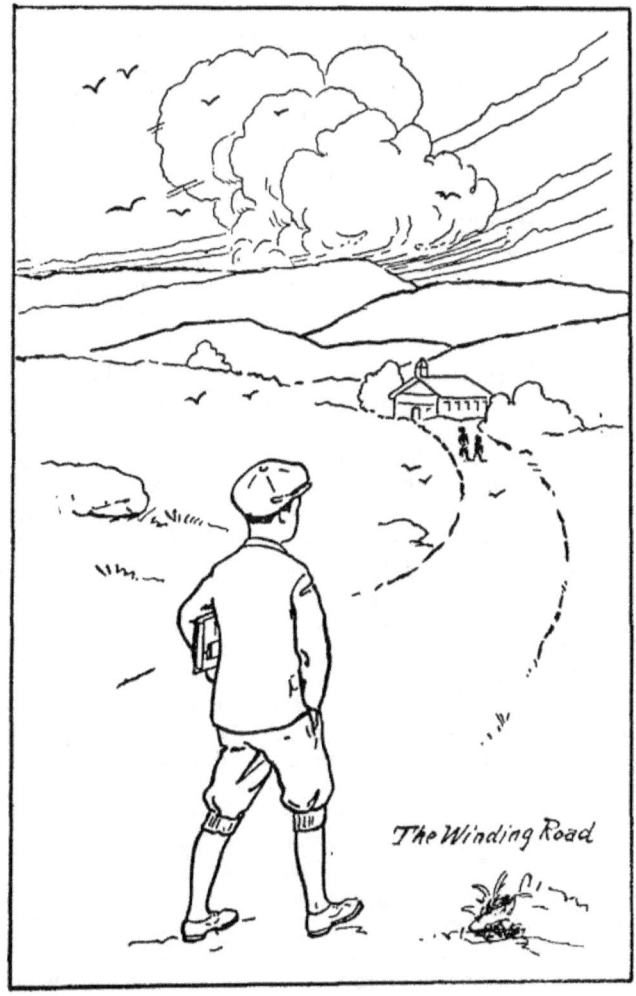

The comparative size of objects and the few simply placed lines are what gives proper perspective to this picture.

HOW TO PRINT CORRECTLY

It is surprising to see how few people there are, even among those who are well educated and well read, who know how to print letters properly. This is attributed to a lack of attention. Any person who desires to print some words on the board occasionally with a picture or diagram should know how to make letters correctly. This is especially the case if the drawing is being done before a class of sharp-eyed pupils.

Most of us pay very little attention to the individual letters when we read; for many it would be a real task to make the whole alphabet in capitals and small letters correctly.

Many times one sees along the roadways or in villages small signs made by amateurs, in which the letter S is made backwards, or some other letter or figure is made incorrectly. Even in such a case many people are conscious that something is wrong, although they cannot say just what it is.

The Roman letters, the type of letters used in our ordinary reading, have what are called a shaded line and a light line. At first sight it may seem that the shading is irregular, or without a purpose. But we should bear in mind that in olden times reed pens were used in making letters, because before movable type and the printing press were invented all printing was done by hand. The vocation of a scribe was considered a profession, and the workman who was good at hand lettering was in demand. As the reed, or flat-pointed pen made of bamboo-like grass, was drawn downward, the stroke was heavy; and when moved upward, it was light, similar to the effect obtained with the use of a pen. The Roman style of letter was fashioned by custom, and for centuries it has been made in the same way.

Take for instance such capitals as A, K, M, N, U, V, W, X, and Y: you can see that capital A, for instance, begins with an upward stroke (light), followed by a downward stroke (heavy)—thus accounting for the light and shaded lines in

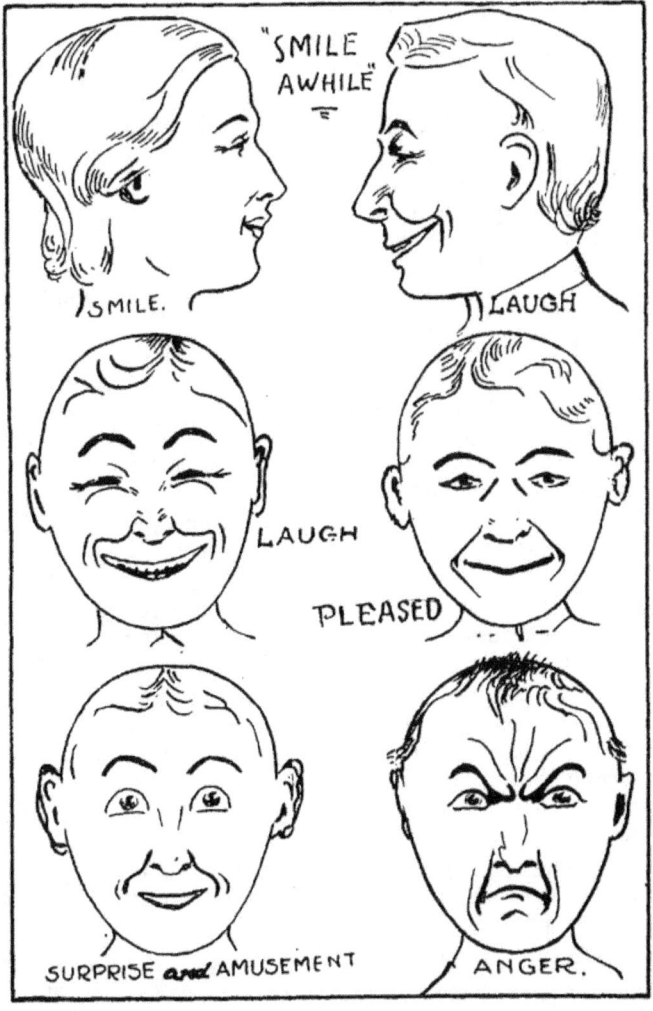

The fewer lines to get the expression the better in chalk talking. Make your marks as nearly as possible like the original. A little further along you will learn more about facial proportions.

the same letter. Capitals M, N, U, V, and W follow this same principle. They seem to have been started at the open end.

The black Gothic style of letter is what printers term "bold face." It has heavy strokes throughout, and the strokes are uniform in thickness.

In outlining your drawing for a printed line, always make light pencil lines for guide lines so that all letters will be of uniform height. Crude letters made uniform in height will pass much easier than perfect letters with no uniformity in size.

Styles of type change with the times; new styles are always being made. Irregular or freakish letters should be avoided; plain letters that anyone can read are the best to use in demonstrative work. An ornamental initial, a colored line underneath a word, or different colors of crayons are often employed for emphasis.

It is well to spend considerable time practicing the proper shapes of letters, until a fairly accurate knowledge is obtained of any particular style of lettering.

Words in which small letters are used are more easily read than words composed entirely of capital letters, and with a little practice they can be made quite easily.

By a little study of advertisements one can see how the different styles of type are employed. Some are wide, and are called "extended." Others are narrow, and are called "condensed"; the latter are used when a considerable amount of wording must be placed in a given line. The heavy-stroked letters are more generally used for emphasis.

An ordinary amount of white space should be around any line of lettering, as crowding destroys the effectiveness of the wording, regardless of where it is.

In making capital letters all the letters are of about the same width, except M, and W, which are wider, and I and J,

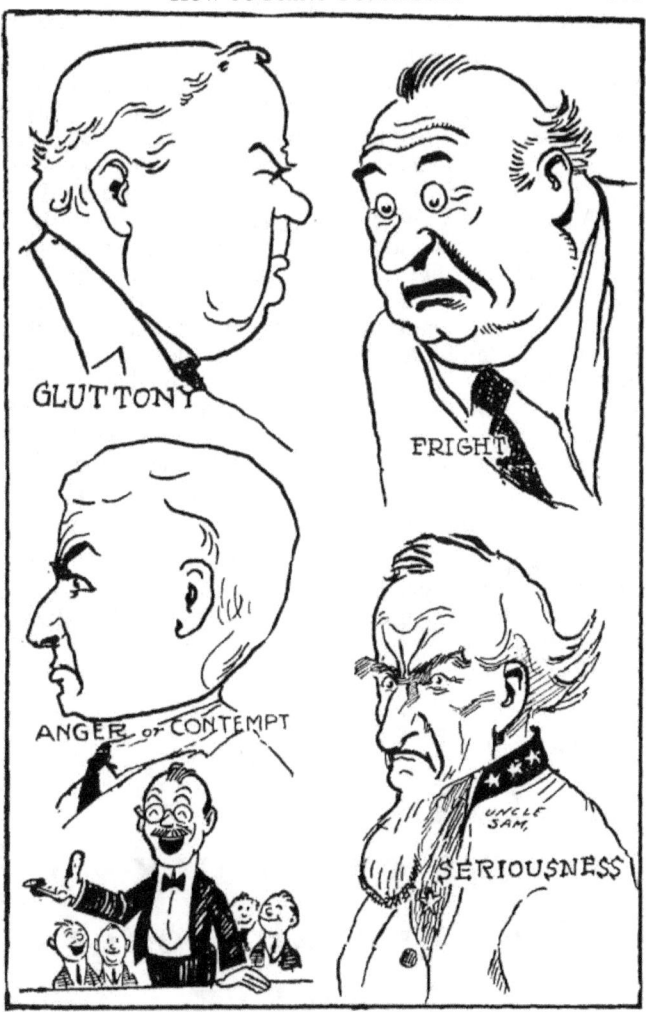

Too many lines will ruin a chalk-talk picture. The right line in the right place is all important. Practice Uncle Sam until you can make him well. You will find his picture always a popular number in general programs.

which are narrower. The horizontal line in B, E, F, H, P, and R should be a little above center, so as to keep the letters from appearing top-heavy. Letters ordinarily should be about the same distance apart; but when such letters as A, V, L, and Y appear in a word such as "VAINLY," in order to give an appearance of uniformity, less space should be between the V and A, and L and Y. Where two letters with full stroke sides, as HI or MN appear side by side, a little more space should be allowed than with such letters as CG, O and S. Capital O, C, G, and Q should be made a little taller than the straight letters (the extension to be both on top and bottom), as they will appear to the eye to be shorter when made the exact height of other letters. The space between words should be about the same as the width of an ordinary letter. Try to keep the perpendicular lines the same angle, as nothing *is* so noticeable as some letters leaning one way and others leaning another.

With a little care the average person will make very good success with lettering.

A few alphabets are here given, so that you can get a general idea of the shape and contour of the letters. It is well to note carefully the heavy and light strokes of the different letters on page 103.

A B C D E F C H
I J K L M N
O P Q R S T U V W X Y Z
a b c d e f g h i j k l m n o p q r s
t u v w x y z

Bold Face type.

ABCDEFGHI
JKLMNOPQR
STUVWXYZ
1234567890&$
abcdefghijklm
nopqrstuvwxyz

Roman type.

ABCDEFGHIJKL
MNOPQRSTUVW
XYZ1234567890
abcdefghijklmn
opqrstuvwxyz

Gothic type.

SYMBOLS   AND   THEIR   MEANING

There are quite a number of symbols used in architectural design, especially in church and cathedral architecture, that have a definite meaning. A knowledge of these is a great help in crayon drawing.

The next time you visit a fine church building take note of the symbols described in this chapter and see how many of them are used. You will find more used in the designs of the large art-glass windows and gables than in any other part of the building.

The symbol of the cross in its multiplicity of variations has been used in geometrical and architectural design throughout the ages, even before the Christian Era. In the later centuries there was an opportunity of elaborating on the variations in designing coats of arms, ornamental title pages of books, and initial letters, before the art of printing came into general use. In the present century designers of cloth prints, wallpaper, stencil borders, linoleum, oilcloth, and so on, have employed unending variations of the standard designs of the cross, circle, square, triangle, and rectangle. The numerals used in this chapter refer to corresponding numbered illustrations, which should be referred to at the time of reading the text, in order that you may firmly establish in your mind the identity of each symbol. (These begin on page 107.)

The Greek cross (1), with four equal arms, is supposed to have originated in Eden, where four rivers flowed in different directions, watering the whole earth. It was a symbol of religion long before the Christian Era.

The circle (2) is a symbol of eternity, as it has no beginning or end; and the cross within the circle (3 and 4) signifies Christianity bounded or surrounded by eternity—a very beautiful symbol both in meaning and design. Every one of the symbols has its meaning, and the various combinations are marvelous in their construction and interpretation.

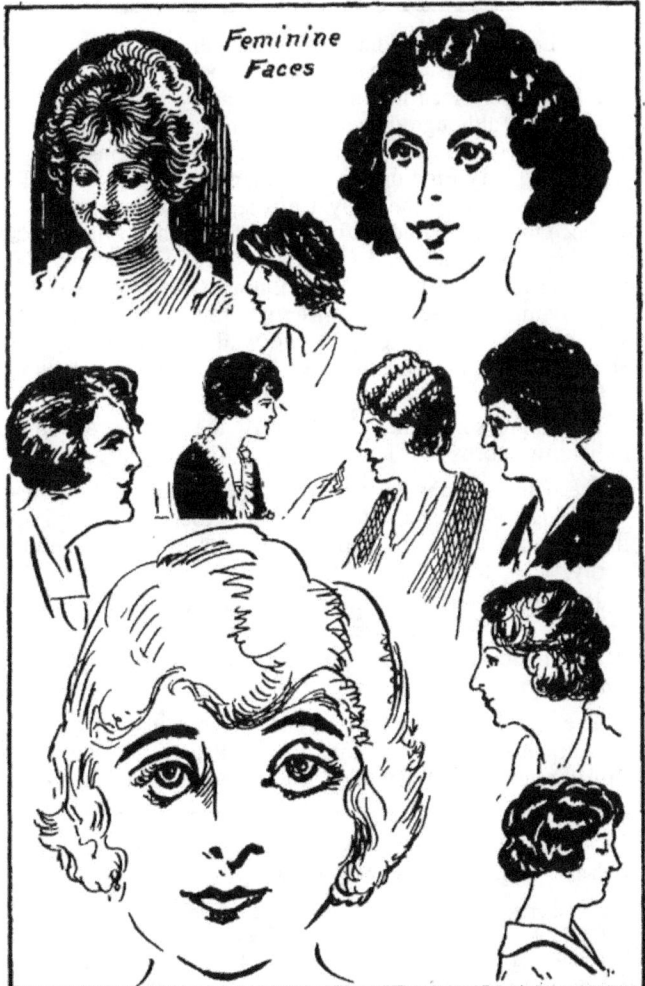

There is no end of the variety of feminine faces. The many ways of hair dressing make a world of difference in even the same model. A good practice is to sketch from living models. Try it. You'll find it interesting.

The Latin cross (5) has a short upper arm and a longer lower arm. This is the type of cross upon which Christ was crucified. Ever since his time the Latin cross has symbolized Christianity, although it was not universally used as such until the reign of Constantine, in the fourth century. Constantine, a pagan, had very little use for Christianity, and added much to the persecutions of the early Christians, until he had an experience that influenced not only his life but that of his mother, and they both embraced Christianity. Then he made it the universal religion of the Roman Empire. In the sky he saw a large, flaming cross, with an inscription in Greek, that was for him what the handwriting on the wall was for Belshazzar. Since Constantine's time the cross has been a universal symbol of Christianity.

In design, sometimes the arms of the cross are pointed, indicating thorns (6). This signifies suffering and sorrow.

The white lily always represents purity, and the fleur-de-lis (7) design in its various forms represents the lily. The lily-blossom design (8) on the arms of the cross is a symbol of purity.

Jewels were used on the arms of the cross (9) to denote value, or priceless treasure.

A budded cross (10) represents life. The form has sometimes been made to resemble a blossom, as well as the bud.

The trefoil (see number 29 and 30 both in text and illustration), meaning the Trinity, or the Father, Son, and Holy Spirit, combines the symbol of Christianity with the Deity.

Explanation of sketch on opposite page. Symbols—In this chapter is material for several programs.

1. Greek cross
2. Eternity
3. and 4. Christianity—eternal
5. Latin cross
6. Christianity—suffering
7. Fleur-de-lis—lilies
8. Christianity—purity
9. Christianity—value
10. Christianity—life
11. Christianity—trinity
12. Saint Andrew's cross
13. Tau cross—Egyptian
14. and 15. Maltese crosses
16. Christianity—light

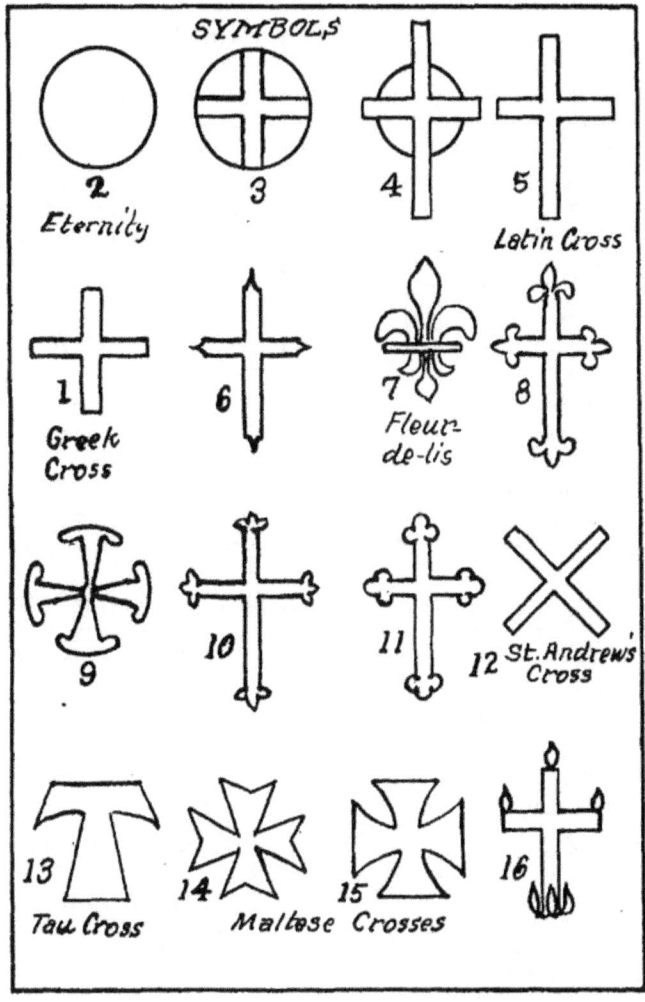

See explanation at bottom of page 106.

The Saint Andrew's cross (12) is like the letter X, signifying the form of death suffered by that Apostle.

The Tau cross (13), so named from its resemblance to the Greek letter T, was more commonly Egyptian. It was used as a religious emblem in India and China before the Christian Era.

The Maltese cross (14) was used in various forms; but authorities tell us that the true Maltese cross is a white cross with eight points, on a black background. It is an emblem of chivalry and knighthood of the Knights of Malta. The commonly used character termed the Maltese cross (15) is also an emblem of knighthood.

A cross with the points burning with flame (16) is a symbol of light, or rather, that one of the attributes of Christianity is light.

Upon a shield (17), which symbolizes faith, the cross represents the connecting link between God and man.

Planted upon a threefold base (18), it is called the Cross of Calvary. The base signifies faith, hope, and love. Faith holds the cross (Christianity), hope underlies faith, and love is the foundation of all.

The cross is sometimes placed on a globe (19) to indicate dominion; it also signifies that Christianity is above the world.

Besides the variations mentioned, there has been an endless variety of combinations used in designs, such as numbers 20, 21, 22, 23, 24, 25, and 26, explanations of which are given below.

Explanation of sketch on opposite page.

More symbols—Good for Church, Sunday School or Young People's Meetings.

17.	Christianity—faith	23.	Christianity—crosslet
18.	Cross of Calvary	24.	Jerusalem cross
19.	Christianity—dominion	25.	Gable cross, Washburne
20.	Patriarchal cross		Church, Worcestershire,
21.	Papal cross		England
22.	Christianity—Gospels	26.	In the Nave of Castle Arch
			Church, Norfolk, England

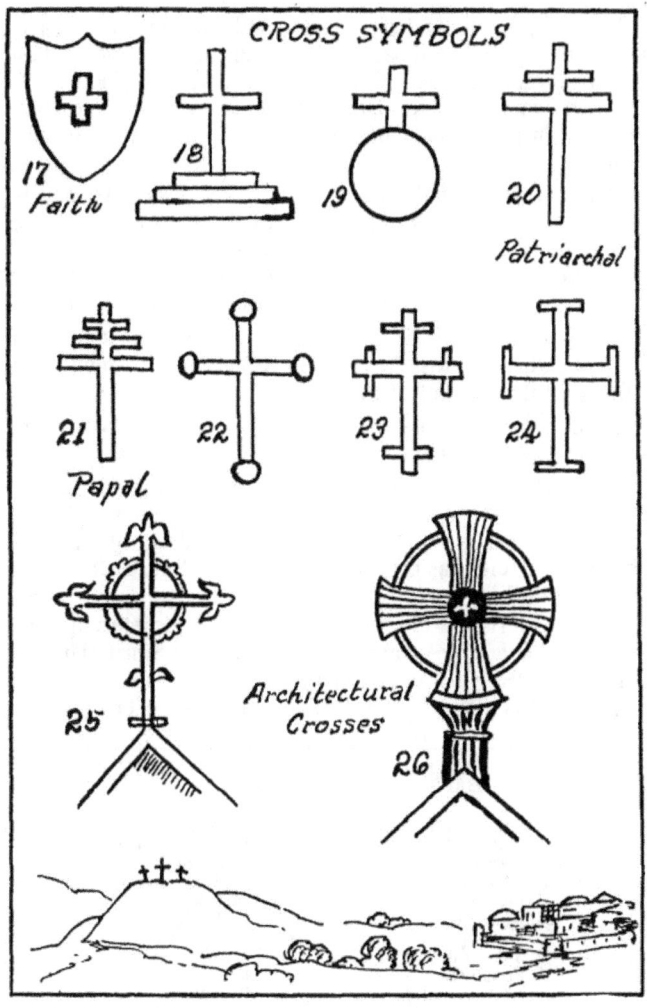

See explanation at bottom of page 108.

With the symbols here represented all the attributes of Christianity in all *its* phases are exemplified; therefore, these significations and meanings lend beauty, knowledge, and character to architectural design. By referring to the illustrations on page 111 a number of added variations will be found.

An entire chalk-talk program for many occasions may be worked out on "The Significance of the Cross," by simply using the suggestions and illustrations in this chapter and enlarging on the various phases. Additional material for the talk may be secured from reference books in any library.

A few songs appropriate for the occasion may be sung, such as "Down at the Cross," "The Old Rugged Cross," and many others on the subject of the cross.

Aside from the cross there are many other symbols, some of which are here given.

Since eternity is symbolized by a perfect circle, the four Gospels and their writers—Matthew, Mark, Luke, and John—are symbolized by four interlaced circles (27). A later form of these four circles has them merged into one figure (28), called the quatrefoil.

Three interlaced circles (29) represent the eternal character of the Trinity—Father, Son, arid Holy Spirit. This design was afterward changed into the trefoil (30). The triangle (31) is also a symbol of the same—the Trinity also

Explanation of sketch on opposite page.

27 and 28. The four Gospels	40. Victory
29 and 30. The Trinity	41 and 42. Peace
31. The Trinity	422. Hope
32. Victory	43. Heavenly wisdom
33. Guidance	44. Sin
34. Message	45. Purity
35. Hate	46. Reward
36. Just punishment	47. Holy Spirit
37. Judgment	48. Church
38. Intellectual light	49. Law
39. Suffering	50. Blessing

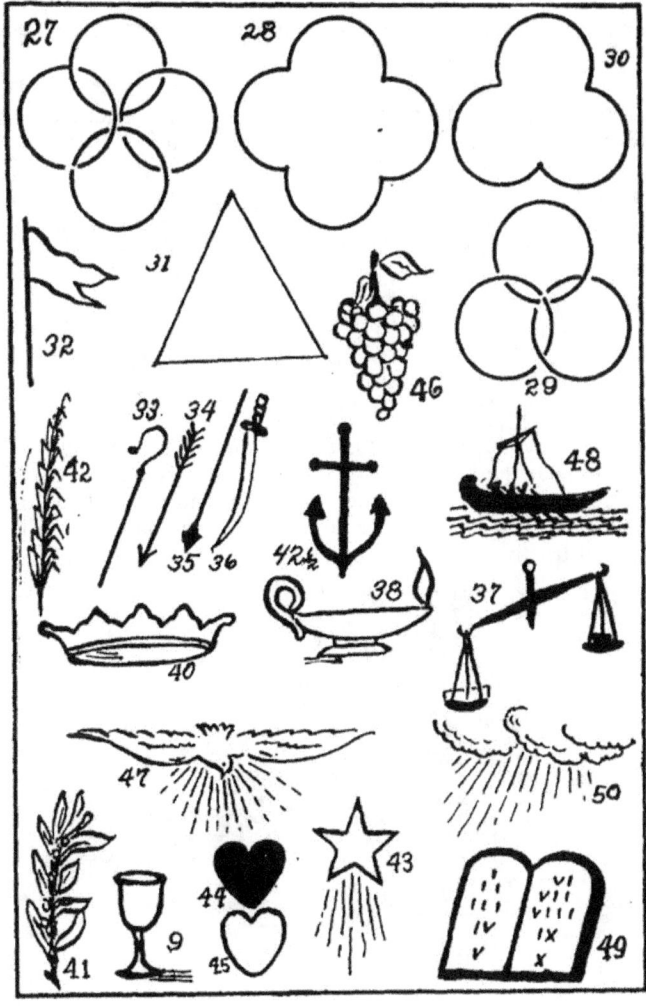

See explanation at bottom of page 110.

denoting threefold unity. The triangle in modern times sig-nifies soul, mind, and body.

Other symbols are the flag (32), for victory; the shepherd's crook (33), for guidance; arrow (34), for a message; a spear (35), for hate, anger, and malice; the sword (36), for just punishment; the scales (37), for judgment; the lamp (38), for intellectual light; the cup (39), for suffering; the crown (40), for victory; the olive branch (41), for peace; palms (42), also for peace; anchor (422), for hope; the star (43), for heavenly wisdom; the black heart (44), for sin, and the white heart (45), for purity; a cluster of grapes (46), for reward; the dove (47), for the Holy Spirit; and the ship (48), for the church. In this case the water represents the world. Law is symbolized by the tables of stone (49) ; and blessing by the rays of light (50) coming through the clouds.

These symbols are but a few of those adopted and used throughout the centuries. Other symbols will present them-selves to the studious worker who desires to get truths to the minds of all ages, as well as to make the chalk talk interesting and instructive.

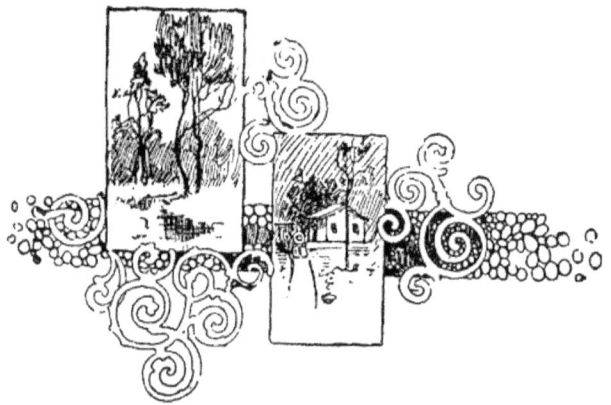

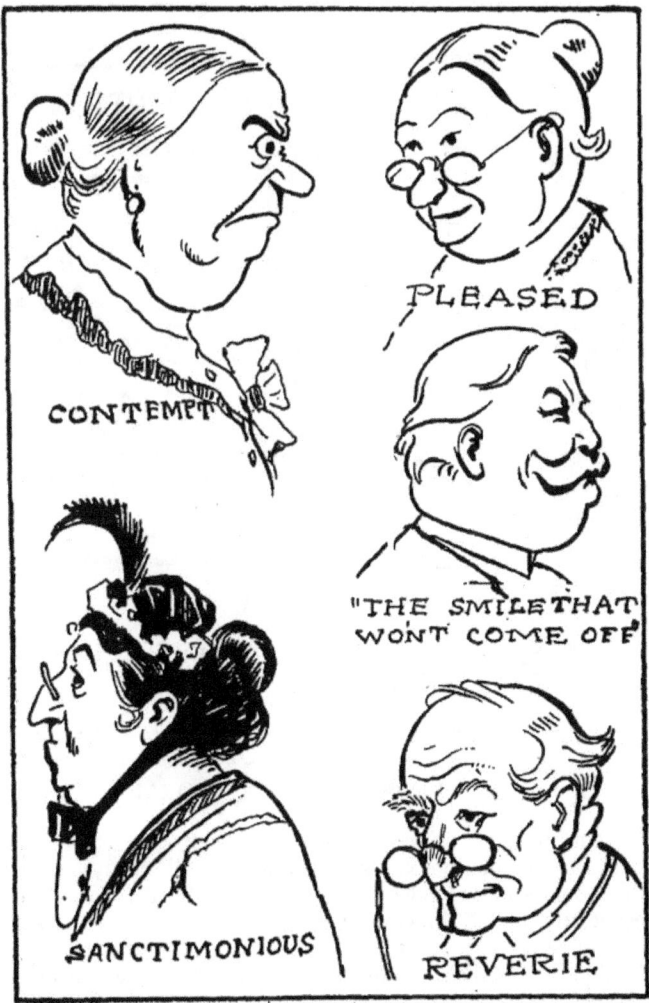

Here we are with faces showing the different moods. Note carefully the markings around the eyes, nose, and mouth. Corners of mouth always turn up when smiling and down when angry or disgusted. Much practice should be put on faces in the different moods.

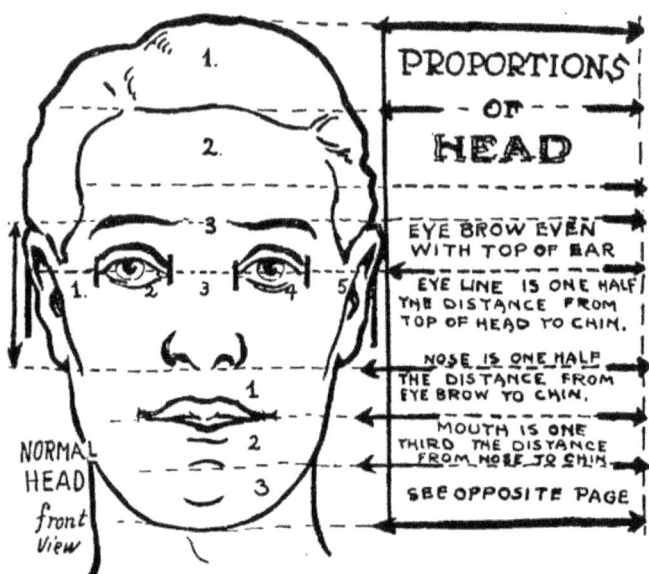

Study the proportions of the head pictured above, and the one on the opposite page. Read carefully, and draw often enough to get the proper proportions in your mind.

DRAWING THE HUMAN FORM

Learning to draw the human form, or any part of it, is a necessity for the chalk talker. The reader will easily tell that this book is not intended to be a complete treatise on art, and especially on the drawing of the human figure; but the suggestions given in the different sketches will be of great value to the interested chalk-talk enthusiast. The simplest forms in representing action are the jets on page 39. The O-shaped

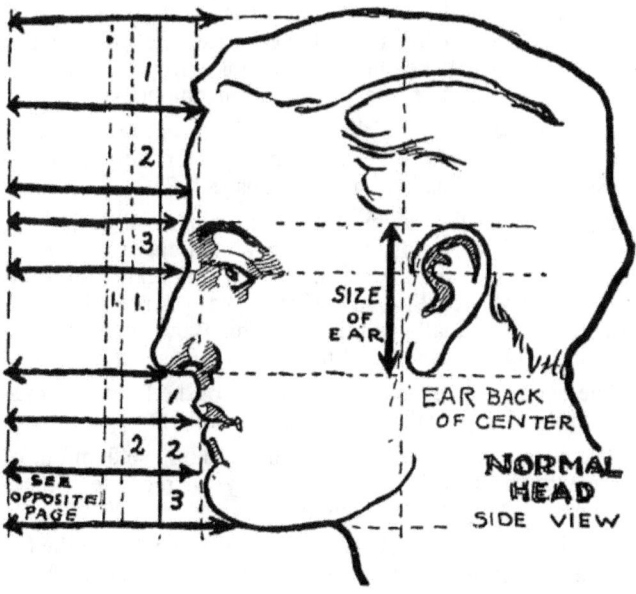

In drawing sketch or cartoon heads, it is not necessary to adhere so strictly to these proportions, but a carefully drawn head always is a mark of knowledge and talent. This chapter should be read carefully.

circle for the head, connected to the legs, can be made to express a surprising multiplicity of bodily actions.

Figures representing the human form are made by cartoonists, artists, and chalk talkers in all sorts of shapes; but in cartoon drawing, the body from the top of the head to the bottom of the feet should not be less than five heads. The correct human figure, however, is from six and one-half to eight heads in height.

The drawing at top of this page shows a normal head. You will see the correct proportions of the face—eyes, nose, ears, mouth, etc.—and the normal view of the body gives a good idea of the correct location of the various portions of the body. Many of the sketches in this book will present to you the lines necessary to express the different emotions.

It is very necessary for the chalk-talk student to be able to portray quite correctly the different types of individuals by the shapes of the head, as shown on page 117.

It is said that the shape of every normal head designates the type of character of the individual and classifies him as one of the six distinct types shown on this plate. You will find a head shaped like an inverted pear—large at the top and tapering gradually to the chin. This type yields more to the comic figure than any of the other types shown.

The opposite type—narrow at the top of the head and wide toward the chin, usually denotes good nature.

The round face is the jolly fat man, who is seldom out of sorts with the world. This face will yield more to the expressions of laughter than any other type.

The long, slim face is the one usually selected to denote the serious-minded philosopher, teacher, preacher type, although it may be used to typify the sort of person who is usually out of sorts with the world.

The square head generally denotes a practical or typical businessman. In cartoons it indicates a man of affairs. The oval type, balanced, common-sensed, having a normal degree of humor, represents idealism and executive ability.

In profile views we again find different types clearly distinguishable by the distinct shapes and contours of the faces. (See same page.)

The first type *is* not stupid by any means, yet is always getting himself into trouble by his habit of acting first and thinking afterward. The concave profile is the opposite to this, indicating habits of thought and concentration. The chin

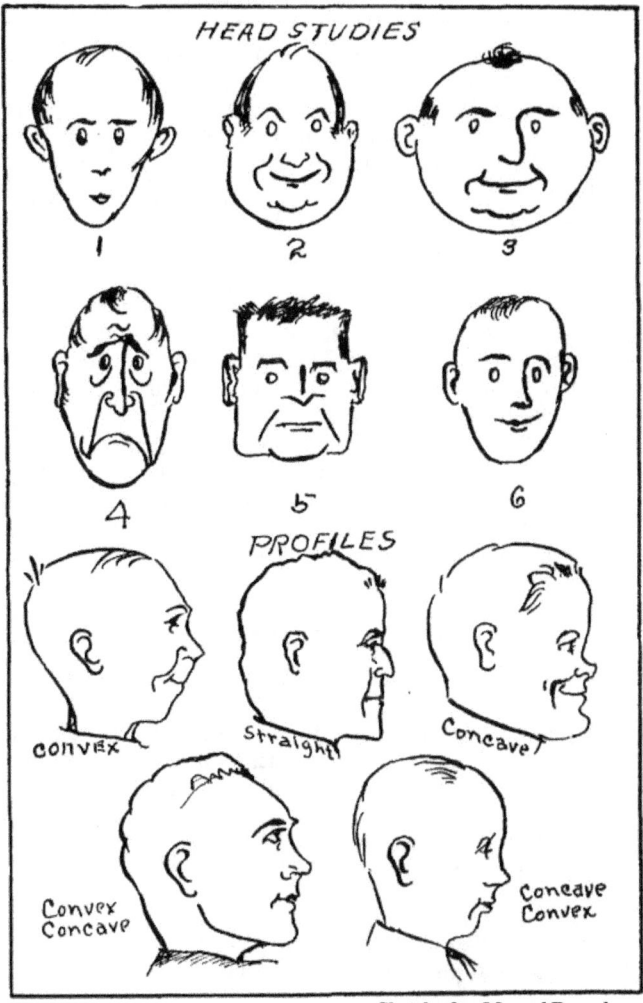

Sketch after Manuel Roeenburg.

It is said that 90 per cent of the normal heads come under one of the types shown here. It is well to make a careful study of these and read carefully the chapter, "Drawing the Human Form."

shows determination and stick-to-itiveness. He usually carries through whatever he sets his head on.

The straight type is the good businessman and executive, calm in temperament, with a mind capable of weighing facts. Firmness and power are indicated in the square chin.

The convex-concave type often includes clergymen, actors, writers, and artists. The strong nose and chin indicate idealistic temperament and a man given to thought and introspection.

The concave-convex type denotes strong thinking power, but weakness in making decisions and carrying projects through to their conclusion. This is the type of person who is always getting into hot water, from which he lacks the resolution to extricate himself.

It is well to note carefully the simplicity of the lines in the face denoting emotion. The turning up of the corners of the mouth is a big start toward a smile, while being "down in the mouth" brings the opposite effect. In fact, expressions are but a trick of line arrangement, as you will notice in the different sketches in this book.

PROPER PROPORTIONS OF THE HUMAN BODY

In making an ideal human figure there are certain proportions that should be followed in order to have the picture seem natural. The following is the front view of the ideal man's figure:

Top of head to chin, one head.

Chin to breastbone, one head.

Breastbone to navel, one head.

Navel to center, one head.

Center to just above kneecap, one head.

Just above top of kneecap to beginning of calf, one head.

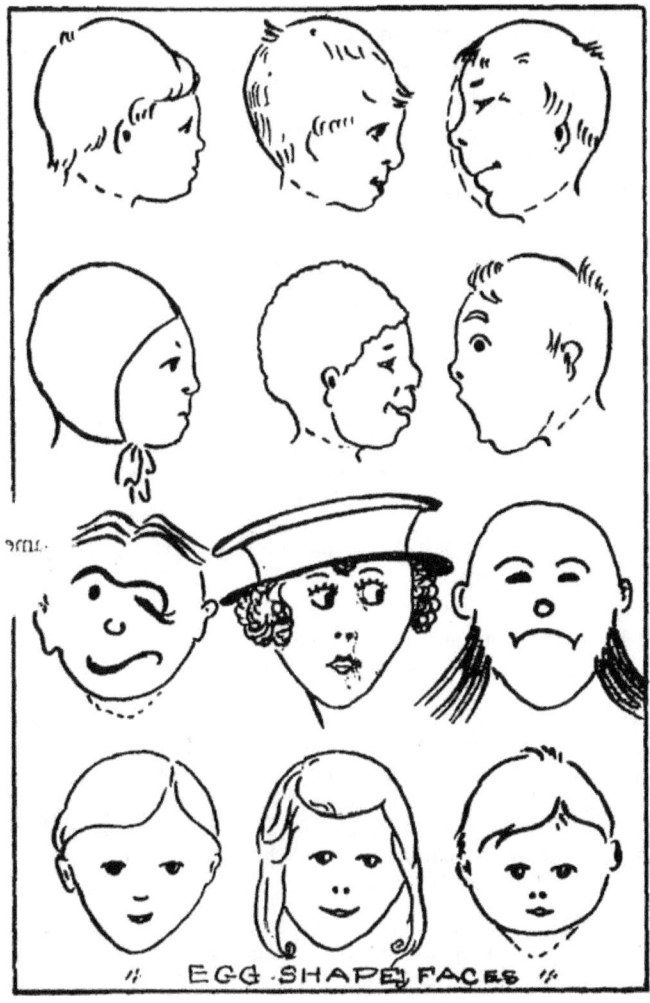

EGG SHAPED FACES

The simplest shape of the front view of the face is the egg. Ears may be omitted without destroying good effect. The hair standing up adds to the expression of fright.

From thence to base of calf, one head.

From base of calf to sole of foot, one head.

Total, eight heads.

The foot is one-sixth the length of the figure.

The hand is three-fourths the length of the head.

The ankle is one-fourth of a head across.

The calf is a little more than half a head across.

The knee at both top and bottom is half a head wide.

The thigh at the widest point is three-fourths of a head in width.

The waist is one and one-fourth heads wide.

The shoulders are two heads wide.

The neck is half a head high.

The comparative divisions in the height of an ideal woman's figure are substantially the same as those of an ideal man, but the widths are considerably different.

The foot, ankle, calf, knee, and thighs are nearly the same as those of the man.

The hip is two heads across.

The waist is one and one-eighth heads wide.

The shoulders are one and one-half heads across.

The neck is half a head wide.

The front head is egg-shaped, the smaller end being at the base. Please note carefully the proportions of the head on page 114. The eye is divided into three equal parts, of which the pupil is the central one. The eyes are the width of one eye apart; the ear is as long as the nose; and the mouth is a little wider than the eye.

The center of a baby's figure is at the navel. A child of about three years is usually five heads high; the upper part of its figure is three heads, the lower part two. A child of six years is six heads high.

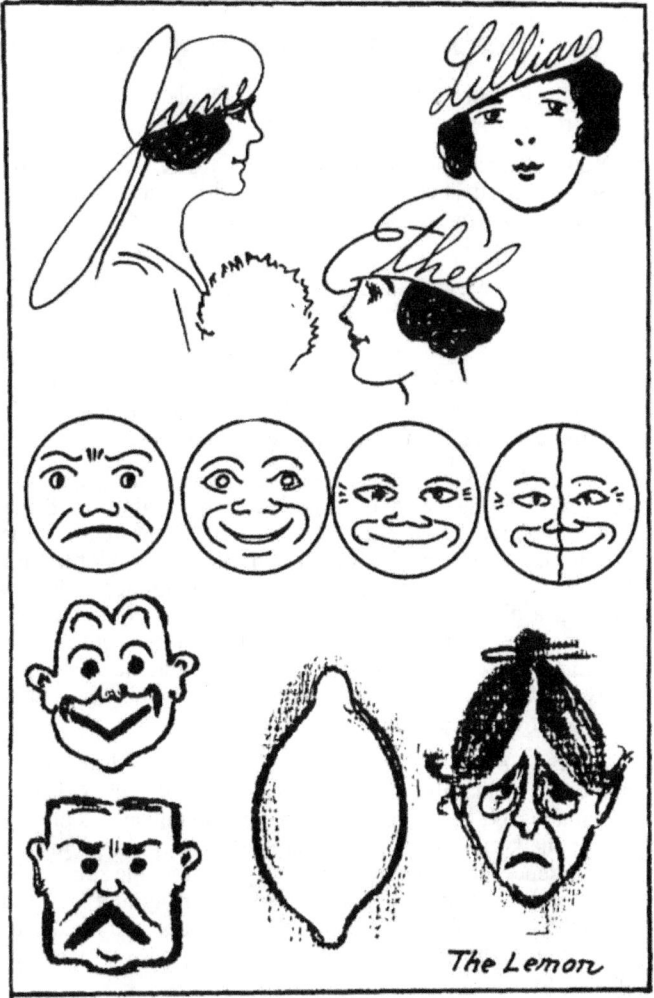

The three upper figures are but simple manipulation of names and faces. Note the effect of the perpendicular line in the moon face on the right. It is the same face as the next one to it. The figures on the lower left are what are termed the Right and Wrong Angles.

CHALK TALK USED IN TEACHING

Scientists claim that nothing which completely occupies the mind for any length of time is ever forgotten.

You can remember incidents and pictures seen in childhood, or something illustrated in connection with what has occupied your attention for some time, and these scenes are never forgotten.

Through the eye, our mind is said to receive impressions that are more lasting than those received through any of our other senses.

Pictures may be ever so beautiful, and yet not give a lasting impression; but an appeal to both the eye and the ear marks the highest development in the methods of teaching truth.

The chalk-talk method of teaching is lasting and impressive. A speaker or teacher may stand before his class or audience and use the most eloquent words, and still his hearers may not be interested. He may resort to a graphic word picture, and he will detect an increased amount of attention; but let him pick up a piece of chalk, and everybody is interested, for the audience expects him to do something. When curiosity is added to interest, the minds of those in the audience become active and ready for the impression that the speaker has within his power to make on them.

Every line made by the chalk, therefore, is full of interest; and every chalk talker knows the value of just such a situation and makes use of it. That *is* just the reason that at this point so many chalk talkers make what are called surprise pictures. If the audience is disappointed in its expectation, the speaker has lost a point; but if the chalk is used to portray and fulfill the meaning of the word picture, both the message and illustration have made the point, and a lasting impression has been made.

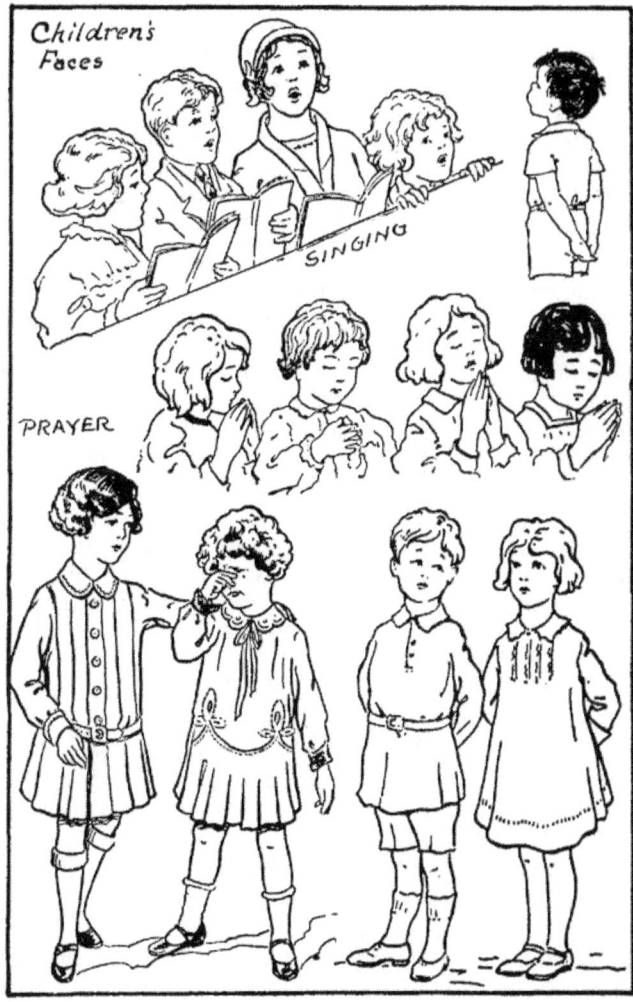

Children depict their emotions and characteristics in the open-window manner. Here are several good children's poses. Sketch them and then try to sketch some living models.

People may seem to forget everything else while watching a speaker draw a picture; but they will never completely forget the point if well made. The young, as well as the old, can read pictures; in fact, pictures are a universal language. They are like the smile which can be understood by human minds of different nationalities. The modern moving picture has demonstrated this fact in getting information and facts to immigrant population when attempts through unknown languages were futile.

Any person telling a story or describing a scene is in reality drawing a word picture for his hearers; and the more realistic the description, the more perfectly the picture is impressed on the mind, especially when a chalk picture is included. Well do I remember certain teachers, both in public school and Sunday school, who knew the art of picturing scenes and incidents so vividly that the deep impressions they made in my childish mind are just as fresh as if they were received but yesterday.

Teaching by such methods is an art almost as old as the history of man. It was the one great method used by Christ, who was acknowledged by the learned people of his day to be the Great Teacher. Men of his own time were compelled to admit the power of his teaching; even the chief priests admitted that "never man spake like this man."

Christ's parables were word pictures of the most vivid clearness. The stories of the Good Samaritan and the Prodigal Son are known to almost every intelligent person. They are pictured in the mind's gallery in as realistic fashion as if photographed or painted there.

Christ's parables of the Lost Lamb, the Lost Coin, the Sower, the Fig Tree, and the Vineyard are illustrations that are vivid and realistic. When he gave the word picture of the shepherd leaving the ninety-nine sheep, which were safe in the fold, and going out into the night to find the one that had

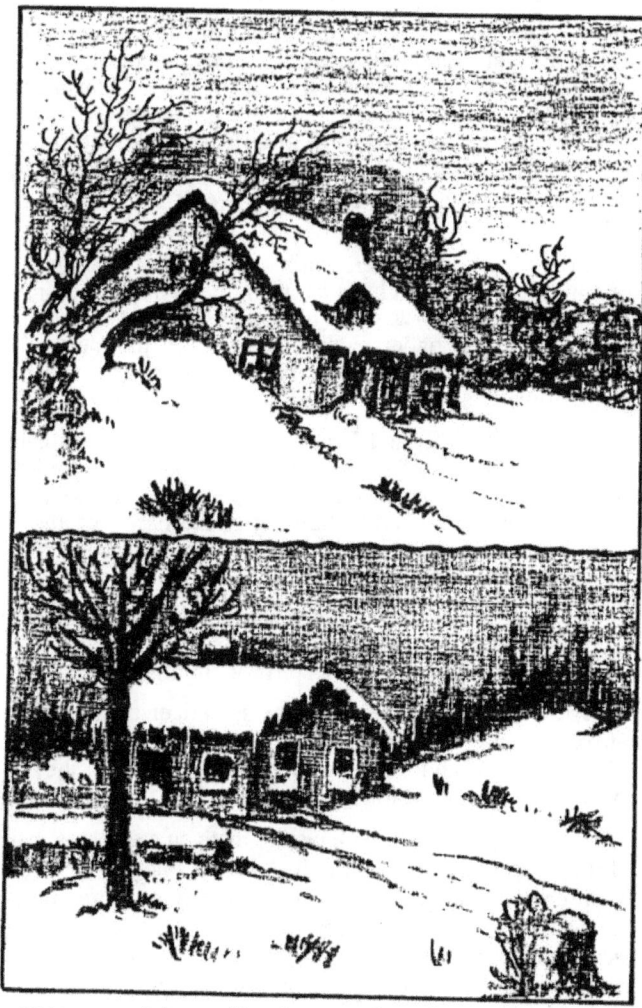

Either one of these will make a good number on your chalk-talk program. The beauty of a snow picture is that the prominent part of the picture is the paper. If you use this as a number on your program, save it for near the close.

strayed away and was lost, he demonstrated a panorama of vivid realism. Shepherding was a common occupation in those days, and nearly everyone knew of it. Many people nowadays would not understand a story of the same kind so well; but if the speaker were to use the chalk and draw a sketch of the sheepfold, of the shepherd going to hunt the lost sheep, and the finding of the lamb, the lesson would be just as real.

Christ's life as a teacher, and his methods, are well worthy of emulation. He must have been an interesting talker, in his original and winning way. He used words and illustrations that the people could understand in order to get the message to them, as, for instance, asking the woman of Samaria for a drink of water and then telling her about the living water.

It was while Peter and James were fishing that Jesus called them to be fishers of men; and after the five thousand had been fed, Jesus declared himself to be the bread of life. Also, when the people were all thinking of the Passover and the slain lamb, Christ told his disciples that his own body would be broken and his blood spilled for the sins of the world.

The great reason for Christ's words making such a lasting impression upon both old and young was his tactful method, as well as the accompanying spirit of simplicity.

It behooves all who wish to impress truth on their hearers to strive to apply the same tactics and methods as those of the Great Teacher; and by the wise use of the crayon, they can make lasting impressions on the hearers.

Any blackboard or crayon picture that you are able to make, if it does not have a lesson in it—if it does not impress some truth or cause someone to think differently or more nobly—misses the mark, and misses it badly. But when the chalk accompanies and impresses your point it acts as a climax and rivets the lesson on the minds of the hearers.

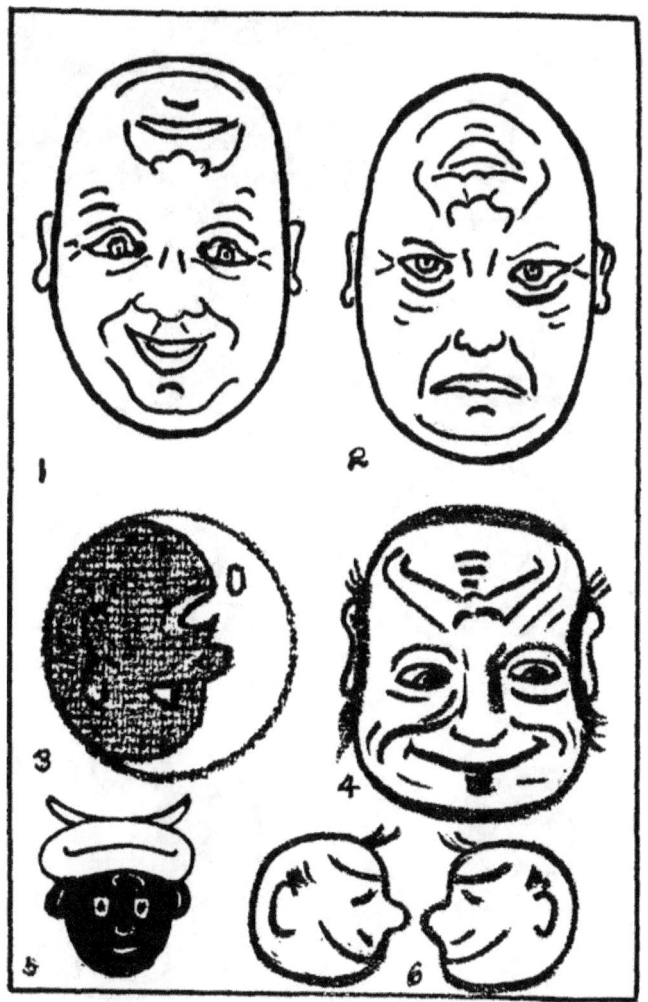

TURNOVER STUNTS—1. Sunshine. 2. Shadow. 3. Light and dark of the moon. 4. The two-faced man. 5. Mandy and Rastus. 6. Two of a kind.

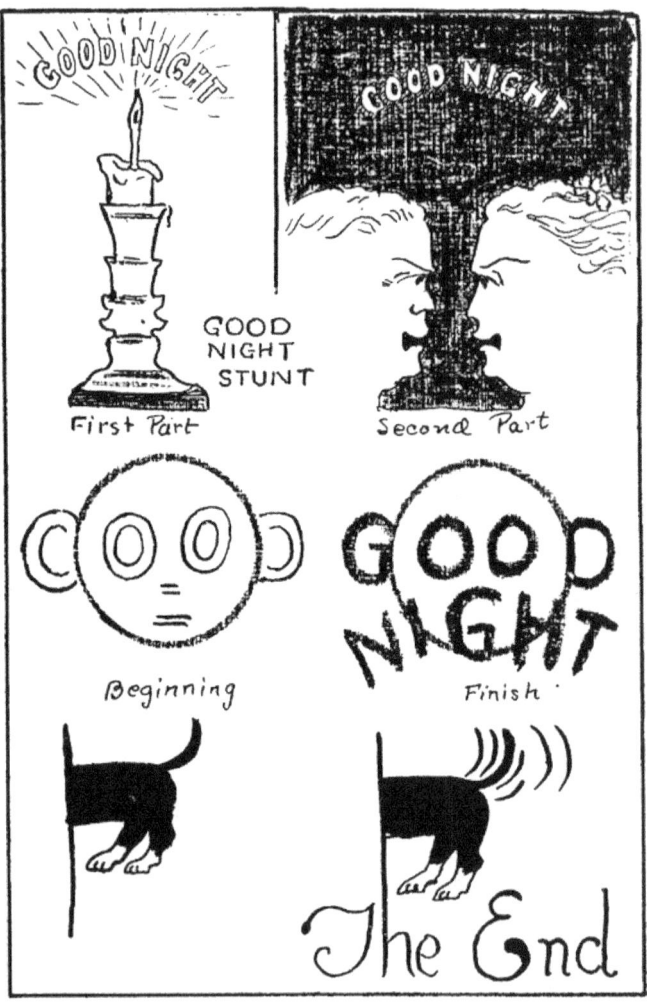

There are a number of "Good Night" stunts, of which only two are here given. You can easily adapt your own from almost any sketch.

129

Also available from www.sunvillagepublications.com

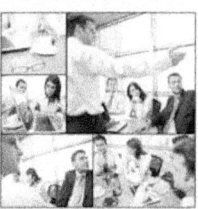

BRAIN STORMING

The Dynamic Way To Create Successful New Ideas

Charles H. Clark

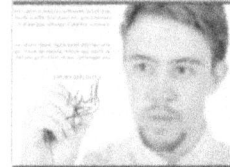

How To Write SUCCESSFUL BUSINESS LETTERS In Just 15 Days

John P. Riebel

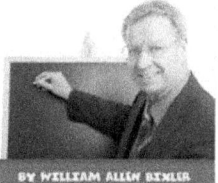

CHALK TALK MADE EASY

A COMPLETE SELF-INSTRUCTION COURSE IN CRAYON AND BLACKBOARD DRAWING

BY WILLIAM ALLEN BIXLER "THE RILEY ARTIST"

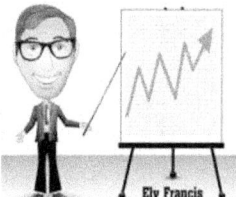

USING CHARTS TO IMPROVE PROFITS

Ely Francis

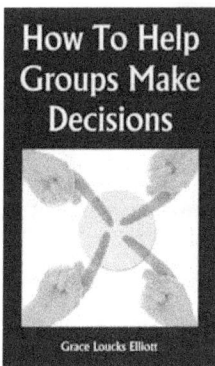

How To Help Groups Make Decisions

Grace Loucks Elliott

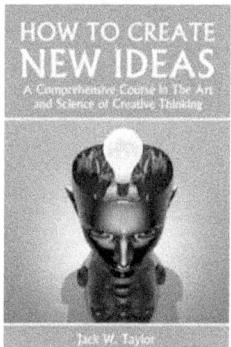

HOW TO CREATE NEW IDEAS

A Comprehensive Course in The Art and Science of Creative Thinking

Jack W. Taylor

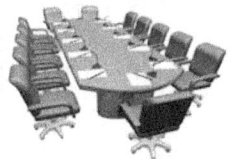

How To Plan Meetings

And Be A Successful Chairperson

Joseph G. Glass, PH.B., LL.B.

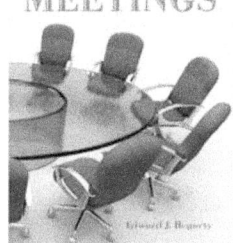

How To Run BETTER MEETINGS

Edward J. Hegarty

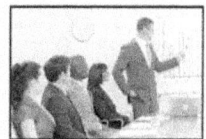

The Successful Sales Meetings Handbook

Bill N. Newman

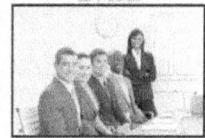